DESCRIPTIVE CATALOGUING

A students' introduction to the
Anglo-American cataloguing rules 1967

DESCRIPTIVE CATALOGUING

A students' introduction to the
Anglo-American cataloguing rules 1967

JAMES A TAIT
MA FLA

F DOUGLAS ANDERSON
ALA

of the department of librarianship at the University of Strathclyde

CLIVE BINGLEY LONDON

FIRST PUBLISHED 1968 BY CLIVE BINGLEY LTD 16 PEMBRIDGE ROAD
LONDON W11   SET IN 10 ON 11 POINT PLANTIN AND PRINTED IN GREAT
BRITAIN BY THE CENTRAL PRESS (ABERDEEN) LTD   COPYRIGHT ©
JAMES A TAIT & F DOUGLAS ANDERSON 1968   ALL RIGHTS RESERVED
85157 056 9

CONTENTS

ACKNOWLEDGMENTS The authors wish to thank the Library Association for permission to base this work on *Anglo-American cataloguing rules—British text*, London, 1967.

Acknowledgments are also due to the following publishers for their permission to reproduce the title-pages used for the worked examples:

Heinemann Educational Books Ltd	— example 1
Macmillan and Co Ltd	— examples 2 and 9
Jonathan Cape Ltd	— examples 3 and 16
Dover Publications Inc	— example 4
Oxford University Press	— examples 5 and 15
The Brookings Institution	— example 6
Prentice-Hall International Inc	— example 7
John Wiley & Sons Inc	— example 8
Pergamon Press Ltd	— examples 10 and 17
Agon Elsevier	— example 11
University of California Press	— example 12
William Heinemann Ltd & A D Peters & Co	— example 13
Feffer & Simons Inc	— example 14
Her Majesty's Stationery Office	— examples 18, 22, 23, 24 and 25
US Government Printing Office	— example 19
Clive Bingley Ltd	— example 20
Hutchinson & Co (Publishers) Ltd	— example 21

PREFACE

With the publication of the *Anglo-American cataloguing rules—British text* in December 1967, the authors felt that students of practical cataloguing would benefit from an introductory text to the new code, outlining its main provisions.

No attempt has been made to cover the code in its entirety. The structure of the new code with its emphasis on basic bibliographical conditions itself makes detail unnecessary. Once the main rules are understood by the student, he is expected by the code itself to apply these to particular cataloguing problems or types of publication.

We have exercised even greater selectivity by omitting those sections of the code dealing with rules for special materials other than those for monographs. The facsimile title pages have two uses: to illustrate the problems dealt with by the text; to serve as a basis for the entries which follow.

The student, if he wishes, can use the facsimile title pages for practice in cataloguing if he ignores the specimen entries. The entries are the authors' own interpretation of the rules, and opinions may differ on details, but it is hoped they exhibit the consistency necessary for all good cataloguing.

Although emphasis has been laid on the value of the book to students of practical cataloguing we feel it may also be useful to librarians as a general introduction to the new code.

J A T
F D A

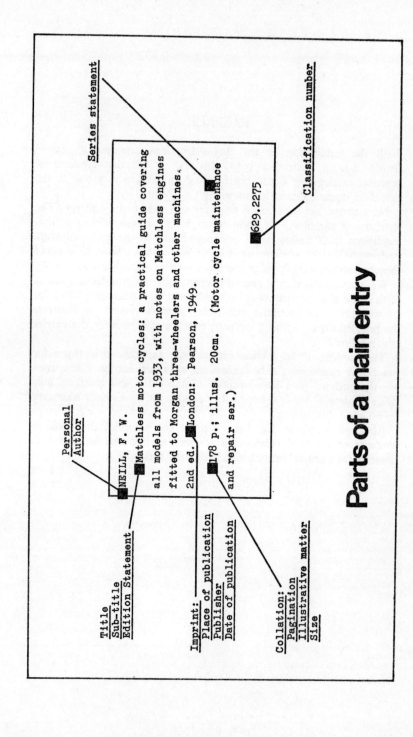

Parts of a main entry

Title
Sub-title
Edition Statement

Personal Author

Imprint:
Place of publication
Publisher
Date of publication

Collation:
Pagination
Illustrative matter
Size

Series statement

Classification number

NEILL, F. W.

Matchless motor cycles: a practical guide covering all models from 1933, with notes on Matchless engines fitted to Morgan three-wheelers and other machines.
2nd ed. London: Pearson, 1949.
178 p.; illus. 20cm. (Motor cycle maintenance and repair ser.)

629.2275

HISTORICAL INTRODUCTION

Descriptive cataloguing, as contrasted with other forms of cataloguing, such as subject cataloguing, analytical cataloguing etc, refers to the process of describing a book or other document in a catalogue entry. To arrange the description of a book in the catalogue, a ' heading ' must be supplied, *ie* a name, word, phrase, or other symbol which will determine the place of an entry in the sequence of entries in the catalogue. As the basic catalogue in most libraries is usually considered to be the author catalogue, this textbook is concerned with author/title cataloguing only. To be efficient, and to be used successfully, any catalogue must be consistently compiled, and the items it lists must be consistently described. The descriptive cataloguing to be described in this book is based on the recently published *Anglo-American cataloguing rules: British text*, published by the Library Association in 1968, but with the imprint date 1967. This is a very complete code of rules for author/title and descriptive cataloguing, and no attempt will be made to cover all the detailed instructions in the 1967 code. Only the most important rules of description, and for entering under author and title will be alluded to. The 1967 code also contains detailed rules for cataloguing certain types of non-book material. These have also been excluded from the present book, which is in no way a substitute for the complete code; it is rather an interpretation and explanation of the more important rules. The new code is an international code, having been prepared by the American Library Association, the Library of Congress, the (British) Library Association, and the Canadian Library Association. The Americans issued their text in January 1967. While both texts are generally in agreement, there are points of difference, and these will be noticed as the points are dealt with.

The *Anglo-American cataloguing rules* is a code of rules dealing with the description of books and other documents, and the entering of them under the names of their authors, or, in the absence of authorship, under their titles. So far as this country is concerned, it is the first new official code to be published since 1908, when the previous official code: *Cataloguing rules: author and title entries* was published. The 1908 code was a similar joint production of the British and the American Library Associations. Unlike the British, the Americans have had several revisions of their cataloguing rules between 1908 and 1967. They brought out a ' Preliminary second

1*

edition' in 1941, followed by the second edition ALA *Cataloging rules for author and title entries; 2nd ed; edited by Clara Beetle* in 1949. In 1960 came their *Code of cataloging rules: an unfinished draft.* This is not to say that other countries have not felt the need for a new code for many years. All sorts of new types of publications, particularly those issued by governments and corporate bodies have appeared and multiplied in increasing numbers and diversity. Libraries have grown larger and more complex. Co-operation in revision took place between the two associations during the nineteen thirties, but the outbreak of the second world war halted further British participation, and it was not until 1956 that the Catalogue Code Revision Committee was able to co-operate again with their American colleagues.

To understand the principles behind the *Anglo-American cataloguing rules* of 1967, and to use them efficiently, some knowledge of the events leading up to their publication is necessary. The code of 1908, while admirable for its time, was based on entirely different principles from the present one. Its basic aim was to give the cataloguer guidance for as many as possible of the specific problems he was likely to encounter. It was based on the practice of providing specific rules for types of publications and classes of persons and corporate bodies. The American 'Preliminary second edition' of 1941 attempted to do the same, but by then the problems had multiplied considerably, and so it was a much larger and more complex code than that of 1908. Like its predecessor, it included both rules for description and for determining the author heading and its form. The rules for description were poorly received in the United States, although there was less criticism of the rules for entry and heading. The American Library Association continued its efforts, which in 1949 resulted in the second edition. This edition did not contain rules for description. The Library of Congress had been revising its own rules for descriptive cataloguing, and in 1949 also published its *Rules for descriptive cataloging; revised edition.* These were adopted by the American Library Association as their rules for description, so that the American cataloguer had, after 1949, virtually two codes to consult—one for description, and one for determining the entry heading, and the form it should take.

The Library of Congress *Rules for Descriptive Cataloging* were generally accepted by the profession, but the same was not true of the ALA second edition. The ALA *Cataloguing rules* were in direct descent from the 1908 code, attempting to enumerate and legislate for all the problems which were likely to come the way of the cataloguer in a large research library. As a result, it was a lengthy and complicated code of rules, and because it was so taken up with specific problems, it often overlooked the fact that specific problems could have much in common with each other in many instances. As a result, many of the specific rules were unnecessary, and were sometimes inconsistent with each other. Exceptions abounded, and even exceptions to exceptions. These exceptions were also often the result of a belief, which many now think mistaken, that it is better to make an exception to a rule if not to do so would result in a heading which would be inconvenient to the catalogue-using public.

The dissatisfaction with the 1949 code resulted in Seymour Lubetzky, then Bibliographic Consultant to the Library of Congress, being asked by the Board of Cataloging Policy and Research of the American Library Association to make a detailed analysis of the second edition of 1949, and especially the rules for corporate authorship. His findings were published in the now famous pamphlet entitled *Cataloging rules and principles: a critique of the ALA rules for entry, and a proposed design for their revision*, 1953. The main theme of Lubetzky's work was that it was a mistake to attempt to provide specific guidance for every particular problem likely to face the cataloguer. Instead, we should look at the conditions that lie behind the problems. In this way, the multiplicity of rules can be reduced and the basic structure of the code made more apparent. Lubetzky's second main point was that exceptions should not be made to rules merely because of the imagined convenience to hypothetical users of the catalogue; instead, a catalogue based on a code of consistent principles would in the long run be more efficient and convenient to use. Lubetzky also brought cataloguers back to the realities of the title-page and the information it contains. Both the code of 1908, and to a larger extent that of 1949, had rules for entry which were based on information not to be found on the title-pages of the books catalogued, but on information discovered elsewhere and known only to the cataloguer, and thus bibliographically irrelevant. Lubetzky's critique is extremely important in the history of the development of author/title cataloguing rules in recent years, and should be read carefully and thoughtfully by all students of cataloguing.

In 1956 Lubetzky was invited by the American Library Association to edit a revision of the 1949 code, and the result was the *Code of cataloging rules, author and title entry: an unfinished draft, 1960*. This gave Lubetzky the opportunity to translate his principles into an actual code of cataloguing rules for author and title entry. The result was a modest code, as one might have expected from the principles. Preliminary discussion of the code by American cataloguers had already taken place at an institute at Stanford in 1958, and the draft code was itself discussed at another institute at Montreal in 1960. The draft code also formed the basis of renewed co-operation between the Library Association in Britain and the American Library Association.

In 1961 an International Conference on Cataloguing Principles was held in Paris under the auspices of IFLA. It was attended by delegates from almost every country in the world in an attempt to reach agreement on the basic principles which should underlie any national cataloguing codes to be produced subsequently. The conference was considered a major triumph in reaching substantial agreement on almost all points, particularly the agreement by the German and mid-European librarians to accept corporate authors as headings. The result was published in 1963 as a report setting out the principles agreed at Paris. The influence of Lubetzky's *Code of cataloging rules* is clearly seen in the ICCP principles, though there were differences in detail.

As both Britain and America played important roles at Paris, it was inevitable that the new code would adhere closely to the Paris 'Principles', which in turn owe much to Seymour Lubetzky. Indeed, Lubetzky himself was editor of the new code from 1956 to 1962, and was succeeded by C Sumner Spalding, who completed the work from 1962 to 1966. The editor in his 'Introduction' specifically states that the rules are based on the Paris Principles. Thus the new code is international not only because it is the joint production of cataloguers in this country and on the American continent, but also because it is largely consistent with an internationally agreed set of principles for author and title entry. Because of pressure from the Library of Congress and the Association of Research Libraries in the United States, faced with large-scale alterations of entries in their catalogues if the Paris Principles were accepted in their entirety, the American text contains some deviations from them which are carefully listed. The British Revision Committee did not always agree with the Americans, and the British text does not contain all the American deviations from Paris. The American text was published before the British in January 1967. Another year elapsed before the British text appeared.

BASIC PRINCIPLES

The *Anglo-American cataloguing rules* are, as their predecessors were, a set of rules designed mainly for the needs of the large research library, although the smaller and less scholarly libraries are taken into account by the provision of alternative rulings when the needs of the latter conflict with those of the former type of library. Such an alternative allows an author to be entered under the various pseudonyms used by him (as the *British national bibliography* already does). Also, the emphasis in this code on more direct simplified headings should make it more attractive to smaller and more popular libraries.

The rules have been designed to meet the requirements of multiple entry catalogues, in which all entries for particular persons or corporate bodies appear under a uniform heading or are related by references, and they provide sufficient entries and references for each item catalogued to be found under the various approaches which might be used by someone unfamiliar with the rules. The distinction is still drawn between *main* entries and *added* entries, *ie* between those giving full information about the item catalogued and those giving less information. The usefulness of the distinction is not so apparent in these days of unit and printed cards, though the concept of one definitive entry for a book or document is important in giving a standard description of a work for library catalogues, and national, book trade and other bibliographies.

In this code, rules are not found to deal with every specific problem; instead the emphasis is rather on types of authorship and classes of names. There are specific rules, but these must always be viewed within the context of the more general rules.

The *Anglo-American cataloguing rules* is a complete code in the sense that it covers both choice and form of entry word and description of the material. It also goes further than previous codes in including rules for a large number of non-book materials likely to be found in a large library—manuscripts, maps, films, prints, records, etc. The rules for choice of entry are almost always kept quite distinct from those for form of heading, which in turn are clearly distinct from those of description. The form of the examples given with the rules is considerably improved. Instead of only giving the entry which would result from the application of a rule, the title illustrating the bibliographical condition covered by the rule is also transcribed.

DESCRIPTIVE CATALOGUING

When we speak of descriptive cataloguing, we refer to the description of the book or document which comprises the main part of the catalogue entry, *ie* all the entry except the heading. The purposes of descriptive cataloguing are two-fold: 1 To identify a book, so that it is easily recognisable from its catalogue entry; 2 To distinguish the work from other works having similar features, and even to distinguish different editions of the same work. Issues or impressions of the same edition are not distinguished. Care must be taken not to confuse the three terms, as they are often used rather indiscriminately by publishers. A new edition implies some alteration in the text, whereas ' issue ' and ' impression ' refer to reprinting from the same plates, without significant alteration in the text. It is assumed that a perfect copy of the book is being described; any imperfections would be noted after the entry.

The title-page forms the main source of the description of a work in a catalogue entry; anything the cataloguer finds it necessary to add to the description is enclosed in square brackets [ ]. In some modern books, the title-page information is spread over two facing pages. In such cases the double page opening is considered the title page, unless two separate titles occupy the two pages. The inclusion of additional material within square brackets does not refer to the edition statement, the imprint or the series statement.

The description consists of two principal parts, each set out in a separate paragraph: 1 Details of the item being catalogued, as generally found on the title-page. These are given in the following order—title, sub- or alternative title, author statement, edition, and imprint (*ie* a statement of the place(s) of publication, publisher(s), and date of publication). 2 The cataloguer's description of the physical volume, phrased in standardised terminology. This appears in a separate paragraph, and comprises the following items: number of volumes/pages, plates, illustrative matter other than plates, size, and the name of the series to which the book belongs, if any. The importance of consistency of terminology and order cannot be too strongly emphasised. A catalogue will be much easier to use if each item described in it is catalogued systematically in a consistent order. The order is laid down for the cataloguer in the rules for description.

TITLE

The title (rule 133): This is to be transcribed exactly as given on the title-page of the work being catalogued. This covers order, wording, spelling, accentuation and other diacritical marks, but not necessarily punctuation and capitalisation. Long titles may be shortened, provided no essential information is lost, and the first words of the title are retained in their proper place. All omissions from the title are indicated by three dots (. . .). If additions are needed to clarify a title, they must be brief and in the language of the title, and also enclosed in square brackets. If the additional information which the cataloguer wants to add is of any length, it should be noted after the entry. An alternative title, *ie* a sub-title beginning with the word ' or ' or its equivalent in other languages, should always be given, because this may be the title by which a person knows a particular work (see example no 2). The sub-title or explanatory title should always be transcribed with the same care as the main title. If it is long and does not supply any further information to that given by the title proper, it may be omitted, and quoted in a note after the entry. A sub-title preceding a title on the title-page should be transposed to its correct position in the catalogue entry, *eg*

Title page reads: An intermediate Textbook/Mathematics for Engineers/.../

This will be given as: ... mathematics for engineers: an intermediate textbook...

Books published without title-pages (rule 132B): These are to be catalogued from the part of the book giving the fullest information. This may be the cover-title, the half-title, caption title, running title, etc. The part used should be specified within square brackets. Works of which the title-pages are missing are not covered by this rule. In this case, the cataloguer should supply the title from some outside bibliographical source, mentioning in a note that he has done so.

Works with several title-pages (rule 132C): A multi-volumed monographic work in which the title varies in all or some of the volumes is catalogued by the title of the first volume. The variations in later titles would be given in a note after the entry. This rule does not apply to serials or periodicals which change their titles.

A one-volume work may also have more than one title-page. In such cases, the code suggests ten possible circumstances in rule 132CI. The more important are as follows. Generally, the first title-page is to be preferred, unless the two title-pages face each other, in which case the second would be chosen. Always prefer the title-page with the latest imprint date. A printed title-page is to be preferred to an engraved one, as the latter may be used unaltered for several editions. If the title-pages are in more than one language, prefer the title-page in the language of the text. Other things being equal, a language preference order is stated—English, French, German, Spanish, Latin, and other languages in the Latin alphabet, Cyrillic, and finally Hebrew. The presence of title-pages not used in the entry should be noted after the entry.

AUTHOR STATEMENT (RULE 134)

The names of authors, whether personal or corporate, are repeated in the transcript of the title, in exactly the form in which they appear on the title-page. The reason for this repetition is to complete the bibliographical description of the book, as the name or form of name used in the author heading may not necessarily be the same as that found on the title-page. The author's name is also repeated in the title-transcript because of the greater importance attached to title-page forms of name in this code, compared with earlier codes. Repetition of the name as found on the title-page enables a cataloguer to determine the form used by an author in his works. However, the repetition of the author's name may be omitted if the form used for the author in the heading does not materially differ from that given on the title-page. It may also be omitted when it is permanently associated with a catalogue entry, whatever the type of entry, as would happen in unit card entry, where the main author heading is always given after the added entry heading and before the title.

Giovanetti, Pericle Luigi
    Nothing but Max, by Giovanetti ...

An author's name may be transposed to come after the title in the title transcript, but not if the transposition would alter the case endings, *eg*

Title-page reads
Konrad Z. Lorenz/King Solomon's Ring/New Light on Animal Ways/...
Transcript would read
Lorenz, Konrad Z.
... King Solomon's ring: new light on animal ways, [by] Konrad Z. Lorenz ...

If the author's name appears only in the imprint, this is adequate as an author statement, without repetition of the author's name in the title (see rule 133C). This will usually apply to corporate authors, *eg*

Title-page reads
Statistical/Abstract of the/United States/ 1966/. . /Prepared under the direction of/Edwin D. Goldfield/ Chief, Statistical Reports Division/. . . U.S. Department of Commerce/. . ./. . ./ Bureau of the Census/.../
Entry would read
United States. *Bureau of the Census*
    Statistical abstract of the United States, 1966 ...
Washington, D.C.: U.S. Department of Commerce, Bureau of the Census, 1966.

If there are more than three authors, all but the first are omitted from the title statement, and represented by the phrase [and others] if the title is in English, and by the appropriate phrase for other languages. In the transcription of personal names, titles of honour, address and distinction are omitted, but not titles of nobility.

Cecil, *Lord* David
    The young Melbourne, by Lord David Cecil ...

Exceptions to the omissions would occur when the designations etc are necessary to identify an author, or to indicate the relationship between a personal author and a corporate body. Additions to the author statement are enclosed in square brackets, for example the word ' by ' which is often omitted from title-pages.

EDITION (RULE 135)
A statement of the edition of a work is included on every catalogue entry for every edition other than the first. The edition statement is

abbreviated and given in a uniform style as: 2nd ed., 3rd ed., etc. It is never written out in full, although the full form may appear on title-pages. If no edition statement is found on a title-page, it is always worth checking the verso of the title-leaf to make certain that it is not there. If it is, it would be included in the title-transcript, without square brackets. If a work is in a number of volumes, and the editions of the volumes vary, this information should be given in a note after the entry. The names of editors, translators, illustrators, etc are included in the edition statement when the work might be identified by them, *eg*

Tocqueville, Alexis de

Journeys to England and Ireland; translated by George Lawrence and K. P. Mayer; edited by J. P. Mayer . . .

Normally details of illustrations are given in the collation, but if the statement of illustrations as given on the title-page gives more information than would appear in the collation, it is repeated in the title-transcript, *eg*

Dickens, Charles

A Christmas carol: a ghost story of Christmas; with the original coloured illustrations by John Leech. London: The Reprint society.

IMPRINT (RULE 139)

The imprint refers to the statement of the place of publication, publisher and date, *in that order*, as normally found on the foot of the title-page, but not necessarily stated there in this order. In the transcript it is given in the language of the title. The date may often be found on the back of the title-leaf; if so it need not be bracketed:

Glasgow: John Smith, 1965.

If a work has been published in several places by one publisher or by several publishers, give only the first-named place of publication and the corresponding publisher, unless some place or publisher coming later in the imprint is distinguishable as the actual place or publisher, in which case this would be preferred.

Imprint reads London/Halton & Co., Ltd./Edinburgh/William Patterson/

Give London: Halton

Imprint reads Pergamon Press Ltd./Oxford. London. New York. Paris

Give Oxford: Pergamon

If a town in the United Kingdom is included in the title-page imprint along with foreign places, it is always included in the imprint, with or without a publisher.

If no imprint is included on the title-page of a work being catalogued, it may be supplied, in the language of the title, in square brackets. A search is made in outside sources if the importance of the work warrants such a search. When cataloguing offprints, separates, and similar material, no search is to be made. The most important item of the imprint is the date, and a search should always be made for it, of which more later.

Place of publication (rule 140) is the place in which the offices of the publisher are situated. The place of printing may be used as the probable place of publication in the absence of the latter. If neither is given, the abbreviation [n.p.] may be used.

Publisher (rule 141): The name of the publisher should be recorded in the shortest form consonant with identification and clarity. The full name of a publisher may be abbreviated to the element representing a proper name, and forenames may be omitted or represented by initials, *eg*

London: Heinemann *for* London/William Heinemann Ltd./
Certain elements in the imprint should, however, be retained. These include:

1 Words or phrases indicating that the name on the imprint is not that of the publisher, *eg*

Glasgow: Printed for the university by Edward Khull . . .

2 Both the publisher and his agent, when both are named, *eg*

London: Published for the British Council, by Longmans.

3. The statement that a work has been privately printed, if a publisher or press is named on the imprint in the book, *eg*

Alva: Printed for private circulation, 1961.

4 Phrases indicating the official status of a government printer, or the official authorisation of a commercial publisher, *eg*

Universitetsforlaget, publishers to the Norwegian Universities.

Date (rule 142): The date given in the imprint is the date of the *edition*, which may be earlier than the date on the actual copy of the book being catalogued, the latter being the date of re-issue or reprinting of the same edition. The latter is added in parentheses when it is considered of sufficient importance, *eg*

1961 (1964 reprint)

    or

1966 (reprint)

when the work is known to be a reprint, and the original date cannot be established. In this instance, the British text differs from the American, and also from the 1908 code, both of which prefer the date of the actual copy of the book being catalogued. The argument in favour of the British rule is that the actual date of issue of a copy of a book which has been reprinted many times over a number of years could give a misleading idea of the date of coverage of the subject by the book. For example if the second edition of a book was published in 1954, and reprinted many times up to, say 1964, if we give the date as 1964, the user of the catalogue might justifiably infer that the up-to-dateness of treatment of the subject in the book is ten years later than it actually is. The British rule also seems more consistent with the principle of describing *editions* only in descriptive cataloguing. It is also more consistent with the practice of regarding the ' work ' rather than the ' book ' as the unit of cataloguing. A footnote to the British text does, however allow those libraries which would prefer to give the actual date of the copy they are cataloguing to do so.

The inclusive dates are to be given for multi-volume works in which the individual dates of the volumes vary.

Dates expressed in calendars other than the Christian era are to be given as they stand, followed by the date in the Christian era in parentheses, in Arabic figures.

Where no date is given on a work, on either side of the title leaf, it is important that an approximate date be supplied, because the date of a work is one of the most important aspects of its description, *eg*

[1963?]—Probable date
[195—]—Decade certain
[18 —]—Century certain.

The copyright date under the 1952 Universal Copyright Convention, may be taken as the edition date; it is usually found on the verso of the title-leaf, preceded by a circled ©. In the absence of a date in the imprint, this may be taken as the imprint date.

In the absence of an imprint or copyright date, a date from any other part of the book should be given. For example, the preface may be dated, and if this is the only date on the book, it should be given thus:

[preface 1884].

The abbreviation 'n.d.' does exist, but it is a poor cataloguer who would resort to this, not even being able to identify the century of publication. Textual evidence should enable one to date a work within a century.

COLLATION (RULE 143)

The collation is the part of the description which describes the physical features of the book being catalogued. It comprises three main elements: 1 The number of pages or volumes, and the number of plates; 2 the principal types of illustration; 3 the size of the volume. This information is given in a new paragraph.

The number of volumes is given for a multi-volume work, and normally the number of pages in each volume would not be indicated. If it was desired to do so, this information would be given as a note after the entry, and not in the collation. Pagination is indicated for a one-volume work by giving the last number in each sequence of paging, leaves, or columns, *eg*

196p./xii, 347p./112 leaves./1540 columns.

Unnumbered pages are generally to be counted, and the total given in square brackets, *eg*

[6], 368p.

Unnumbered pages immediately preceding or following a numbered sequence need not be separately specified if the numbered sequence takes them into account. For example, the half-title leaf, and title-leaf, in modern books, are generally unnumbered, but usually the next numbered sequence takes account of them.

The *Anglo-American cataloguing rules* (British text) would have the following pagination:

xxiv, 327p.

There are four pages unnumbered at the beginning, but the first numbered sequence starts with page v. There are other unnumbered pages, but these are all taken into account by the existing pagination. Given the assumption that any sequence of pagination in a modern work begins on the recto of a leaf, an unnumbered page on the verso of a numbered leaf can be assumed to exist. Thus, in the above pagination, the numbered sequence ends on the recto of a leaf (page 327), and page 328 must exist on the verso of the leaf, but this need not be stated. Pages only containing advertising matter are always ignored.

Included in the pagination is a statement of the number of plates, *ie* pages containing illustrative matter, not included in any of the existing sequences of pagination, and usually printed on a different type of paper than the rest of the volume. For example:

xii, 346p., 14 plates.

This is new, and peculiar to the British text; the North American text leaves the statement of plates where it used to be *ie* with the list of other illustrative material following the pagination (see the North American text, rule 142C1a). Presumably the British Committee preferred the statement of the number of plates with that of the pages because: 1 The plates are outwith the existing sequences of numbered pages; 2 the statement of the number of plates describes part of the physical make-up of the book, rather than a type of illustration.

Illustrative matter (rule 143D): A semi-colon separates the pagination statement from a description of the type(s) of illustrative matter. The abbreviation 'illus.' is used for all types of illustration, unless particular types would seem to be important in relation to the book being catalogued, *eg*

xix, 379p., 12 plates; illus.

Where particular types of illustrative matter are to be specified, they are designated by the following terms in *alphabetical* order: charts, coats of arms, facsimiles, forms, genealogical tables, maps, music, plans, portraits, samples. The authorised abbreviations for these terms are given in Appendix III, pages 285-288.

Where both ' illus.' and types of illustrative matter are stated, the term ' illus.' comes first, *eg*

xix, 379p., 12 plates; illus., geneal. tables, ports.

The presence of coloured illustrations should be noted, *eg* col. illus., ports. (some col.).

The number of each type of illustration should be stated if it is easily ascertainable, and of sufficient importance to warrant mention, *eg*

xix, 379p., 12 plates; 14 illus., geneal. table, 5 ports.

The presence of illustrative matter on lining or end-papers, or in special pockets should be noted, *eg*

xix, 379p.; 14 illus. (7 col.), 3 charts (in pocket), geneal. table (on lining paper).

Size (rule 143E): The third item in the collation is the size of the book being catalogued stated in centimetres to within one centimetre, for books over ten centimetres in height, and for smaller books in millimetres, exact to the nearest millimetre. The height of the binding is measured for bound books, and for unbound pamphlets, the height of the page. For example, 17.2 cm would be given as 18 cm. The width of the book is also given if it is less than half the height, or greater than the height. The height measurement is always stated first *eg*

20 × 8 cm. *or* 20 × 30 cm.

SERIES STATEMENT (RULE 144)

If the book being catalogued belongs to a named series, a statement of the series is given after the collation in the same paragraph. If the name of the series is printed in the book itself, the statement is enclosed in parentheses, if discovered from outside sources, it is given in square brackets. The series statement is kept to a minimum length adequate to identify it, and includes only the title of the series, and the number given to the book in the series. Generally, the name of an editor or author of a series is omitted from the series statement, unless the personal name is an integral part of the name of the series. A series statement or note is essential to identify many official publications, such as ' Command papers ', and the series issued by government agencies, such as the United Kingdom Atomic Energy Authority. If the name of the series forms part of the title of the book, it should, if possible, be omitted from the title-transcript, and given after the collation as the series statement (see example no 5).

Any other information which the cataloguer considers essential to give about a book is given in the form of notes, after the physical description of a book. Notes should be kept as brief as possible—there is limited room on a 5in × 3in card, and the cataloguer should make sure that the notes are necessary, and that they do not repeat information already given in the body of the entry. Notes which deal with a work as a member of an edition are given before those referring to the copy being catalogued; and notes on the bibliographical aspects precede those on the textual scope and contents of a work. Notes may be used to cover the following examples in the order given, though it is extremely unlikely that all or even more than one or two would be needed for any single book.

1 *Notes on the title*
  Caption title
  Added title-page in German

2 *Notes on the author heading or statement*
  Other contributors are:—James Lansdale Hodson, Michael Joseph, W. A. Munford, M.B.E., Cadness Page, [and] Hubert Wilson.

3 *Notes on the edition*
  V.1 2nd ed., 1904; v.2 4th ed., 1910.

4 *Notes on imprint*
  Published by Longmans Green for the British Council.

5 *Notes on the collation*
  Bound with . . .

6 *Relationship to other works, and bibliographical history*
  First published, Paris, 1964.
  Offprint from the Library Association Record, v.69, no.12, Dec., 1967.

7 *Nature, scope, language or literary form of the work*
  Play in four acts
  Text in English and Latin

8 *Contents* (a list of the contents of a work comprising distinct parts by the same author, or contributions by several authors, *eg* collections of plays by the same or several authors. In a multivolume work, the contents of each volume should be stated. The contents should be listed in the order in which they appear.
  New English dramatists, 9; introduced by Michael Billington. Harmondsworth: Penguin, 1966.
  191p. 18cm.
    Contents: A lily in little India, by Donald Howarth.—Skyvers, by Barry Reckord.—The four seasons, by Arnold Wesker.

9. *Notes on the library's copies and holdings*
Manuscript notes by the author.
2 copies.

In the card catalogue of a library it is essential to have on the main
entry card a list of the other headings under which a work is entered.
Such a list is called a list of ' Tracings '. It is needed to trace the other
entries for each book, so that they can be withdrawn when the book
is withdrawn. They will also be needed if some alteration has to be
made to the entry. Rule 146 suggests that the other headings should
be listed in a consistent order, but it does not say what the order
should be. The North American text, in rule 151, lays down an order,
based on the Library of Congress printed card practice, *ie* subject
headings, then added author headings, and then title (if any) etc. Full
details will be found in the American rule. It goes without saying that
the form of the tracings must coincide with the form of the added
entry headings.

CAPITALISATION IN ENTRIES (APPENDIX II)
Very precise instructions are given regarding the use of capitals in
entries. Fairly precise guidance is needed if consistency in capitalisation is to be achieved in the work of one cataloguer, or between the
work of different cataloguers. The rules are taken from the United
States Government Printing Office *Style manual*, revised edition,
January 1967. Certain amendments have been introduced to conform
to current British practice, and some rules have been omitted. For
entries for works in foreign languages, the practice of the language is
followed. For example, in German, all nouns and words used as nouns
are capitalised. Rules for the major European languages are also given
in Appendix II, where the practice in capitalisation differs from that
of the English language.

The first word of all titles is capitalised, and the capitalisation of the
other words in the title is governed by the other rules for capitalisation.
This rule operates as it stands, even if the first word is an article. In
title entries, the word following an initial capital is also capitalised, *eg*
A Taste of honey ...
The first word of a title is not capitalised if the title begins with marks
of omission (see examples 18, 21, 22, 24 & 25).

Within a title, basically, all proper names and derivatives of proper
names are capitalised, *eg*
Scotland *and* Scottish
Rome *and* Roman
However, derivatives of proper names used with an acquired indepen-

dent meaning, or no longer identified with the proper names from which they are derived are *not* capitalised, *eg*

venetian blinds, scotch (whisky), burgundy (wine).

An article within a title is only capitalised if it is an essential part of a proper name, *eg*

At home in The Pig and whistle (inn).

It is not, however, capitalised in the titles of periodicals, newspapers, trains, names of firms, etc, *eg*

A history of the Scotsman newspaper.

The story of the Flying Scotsman.

The words in the names of organised bodies are capitalised, except for articles, conjunctions, and particles, *eg*

Royal Navy.

Her Majesty's Stationery Office.

Geographic names are capitalised, as well as descriptive terms used as proper names, *eg*

the Potteries / the Midlands.

Any title preceding a proper name is capitalised, *eg*

Lord Montgomery.

Captain Hornblower.

The word following a colon, exclamation point or interrogation point is not capitalised, if the matter following merely makes the meaning clearer. In the *imprint*, the first word of the publisher or printer statement is capitalised, and the second also, if the first is an article, *eg*

The Universities press

The items in the collation are not capitalised.

PUNCTUATION (APPENDIX V)

Punctuation marks are used to separate the various parts of an entry. Modern title-pages have little, if any, punctuation, relying on the size and style of type and placement on the title-page to distinguish the various items. The rules for the use of the various punctuation marks which follow are intended to introduce consistency, and to provide clarification.

The use of different punctuation marks enables varying degrees of emphasis to be given between the different parts of the entry. The most emphatic punctuation is the full stop, and this is used between each major section of the entry, for example, between the end of the title statement and the imprint, and between the statement of illustrations and the size. Thus

Down the Clyde, [by] Jack House. Edinburgh:

Chambers, c1959.

Additions to any part of the entry in words or figures, but not punctuation marks, are enclosed in square brackets, unless specified otherwise in the preceding rules. For example [by] in the preceding example. All omissions are indicated by three dots (...). Abbreviations must be marked by the usual full-stop, but not contractions, *eg* 2nd ed. (2nd is a contraction, and is not followed by a full-stop).

Heading: The transposed parts of the heading are separated by a comma, *eg*

Smith, John Henry

The comma is also used to separate a name from a qualifying or identifying phrase or date, *eg*

Smith, John Henry, *watchmaker*

Smith John Henry, 1831-1887

In corporate author headings, a subheading is separated from the main heading by a period, *eg*

Great Britain. *Parliament*

Title and author statement: The title is separated from the author statement by a comma, when the latter begins with a word denoting simple authorship, *eg*

Doctor at sea, by Richard Gordon [pseud.] ...

A semi-colon is, however, used to introduce other types of authorship, such as editorship or collectorship, *eg*

Modern verse, 1900-1940; chosen by Phyllis M. Jones ...

The semi-colon is also used to introduce a statement of secondary authorship (such as translator), except when it forms part of the edition statement, *eg*

Bonjour tristesse [and] A certain smile, by Françoise

Sagan; translated by Irene Ash ...

An alternative title is introduced by a semi-colon, *eg*

Bevis; or, The story of a boy

A sub-title is generally introduced by a colon. There is no ruling on this in the British text, and the examples in the code are not consistent. The *British national bibliography* uses a colon, but the North American text would use a semi-colon for both alternative and sub-title.

Edition statement: The edition statement is separated from the preceding and following statements by a full-stop, *eg*

A Student's manual of bibliography, by Arundel

Esdaile. 2nd ed. London: Allen &

Unwin, 1932.

Imprint: In the imprint, a colon is used to separate the place of publication from the name of the publisher, as in the above example. The name of the publisher is separated from the date by a comma, and a period follows the date, again, as above.

Collation: The statement of pagination and plates is separated from the illustration statement by a semi-colon. A period separates the latter from the size, and this is also followed by a full-stop (see the worked examples).

Series statement: This is enclosed in parentheses (round brackets).

Contents note: Items in a contents note are separated by a period and a dash, as shown in the example previously.

ENTRY AND HEADING

Chapter 1 of the *Anglo-American cataloguing rules* deals with the problem of choosing a heading for the main entry for a work. The words ' enter under ' are to be interpreted as ' make main entry under '. Added, or secondary entries are specified with the appropriate rules, and at the end of the chapter, in rule 33, there is a series of general directions for making added entries. This code attempts to base all its entries on information found on the title-page of the work being catalogued. ' The entry for a work is normally based on the statements that appear on the title-page, or on any part of the work that is used as its substitute '. Sources outside the book itself are only taken into account when a work is published anonymously, or when there is suspicion or evidence that the statements in the work may be erroneous or fictitious.

The order of priority for choice of heading runs as follows:
1 Enter under author, or principal author, when one can be determined.
2 Enter under editor when there is no author or principal author, and when the editor is primarily responsible for the existence of a work.
3 Enter under a compiler *named on the title-page* in the case of collections of works by various authors. 4 Enter under title when the authorship is diffuse, indeterminate or unknown.

So far we have been speaking about ' author ' without defining the term. It is one which is open to different interpretations, and the definition given in the *Anglo-American cataloguing rules* is as follows: ' The person or corporate body chiefly responsible for the creation of a work, *eg* the writer of a book, the compiler of a bibliography, the composer of a musical work, the artist who paints a picture, the photographer who takes a photograph.'

Authorship is based on the ' intellectual responsibility' concept, *ie* the person judged to be primarily responsible for the intellectual content of a work is chosen as author. The definition is also very wide, embracing all the products of creative activity to be found in libraries —books, prints, paintings, music, photographs etc.

WORKS OF SINGLE AUTHORSHIP
Rule 1 deals with the simplest condition of authorship—a work written by one single person. ' Enter a work, a collection of works, or

selections from works by one author under the person or corporate body that is the author, whether named in the work or not.'

Title-page
    The essential writings of Erasmus Darwin
    chosen and edited with a linking commentary
    by Desmond King-Hele.

Main entry under *Darwin*.

Title-page
    Transactions of the Edinburgh Mathematical Society

Main entry under *Edinburgh Mathematical Society*

Title-page
    Historic Houses, Castles & Gardens
    in Great Britain & Ireland.

Main entry under *title*

For the purposes of these rules, a corporate body is defined as any organisation or group of persons that is identified by a name, and that acts or may act as an entity. To exist for the cataloguer, a corporate body must have a name. If authorship is erroneously or fictitiously attributed to someone other than the author, the work is entered under the actual author, with an added entry under the attributed author, if he is a real person. Works of unknown or uncertain authorship, and works by unnamed groups of persons are to be entered under title. The definition of an anonymous work in this code is 'a work of unknown authorship'. This is a description of the knowledge of the cataloguer rather than of the work itself. The 'unnamed group' refers back to the definition of corporate authorship. In certain instances, both the 1908 and 1949 codes allowed the cataloguer to enter under a description of an unnamed group supplied by himself, *eg* Geneva. *American citizens*. The danger with supplying a name to a group or in describing a group lies in the fact that the user of the catalogue may not necessarily use the same description of the group as the cataloguer. A supplied description is also bibliographically irrelevant in terms of the title-page.

WORKS OF SHARED AUTHORSHIP

This group, dealt with in rule 3, covers a large number of works of multiple authorship, where the functions of each author are similar. It includes what was previously known as joint authorship, composite works (*ie* works comprising separate contributions by different authors written for the occasion), and works consisting of an exchange between different persons, such as correspondence, debates, etc. The distinction found in the previous codes between joint and composite authorship is no longer maintained. This is similar to the provisions of ICCP.

The main rule for works of shared authorship (rule 3) is to enter under the person or corporate body to whom chief responsibility can be attributed. Added entries are to be made under the other authors, if there are not more than two, and always under the author whose name appears first on the title-page, if he is not the principal author.

Title-page

Fodor's Woman's Guide to Europe ... Eugene
Fodor Editor. Editorial contributors:
Alyce Martin, Suzanne Cardozo, Sally Brunet ...

Main entry under *Fodor*

In added entries for other authors, phrases such as *joint author* are no longer suffixed to the author's name in the heading. This simplifies the filing of such entries in the catalogue, as compared with the practice of 1908 and 1949.

Where no responsibility is indicated on the title-page, entry is under the first author named on the title-page, provided there are not more than three, with added entries under the other two.

Title-page

Practical Field Surveying and Computations ...
A. L. Allan, J. R. Hollwey, J. H. B. Maynes ...

Main entry under *Allan*. Added entries under the other two authors. If no one is represented as the principal author, and there are more than three authors, entry is under the title, unless an editor is named on the title-page.

Title-page

The English Presbyterians from Elizabethan
Puritanism to modern Unitarianism. C. Gordon
Bolam, Jeremy Goring, H. L. Short, and Roger Thomas.

Main entry under *Title*

Title-page

The Scallop. Studies of a shell and its influences
on humankind by eight authors. Edited by Ian
Cox.

Main entry under *Cox*

The 'rule of three' obviously stems from the observation that the greater the number of names on a title-page, the less is the likelihood that any *one* will be used by an enquirer as the entry point into the catalogue. The abolition of the distinction between joint and composite authorship was long overdue. The distinction was never completely maintained, and the user of the catalogue was very unlikely to appreciate the subtle distinctions between the two types of authorship when looking in the catalogue.

Collections have a rule to themselves (rule 5). These are collections of independent works by various authors, not written specifically for the publication in which they appear. They may have been published previously. If they have a collective title they are to be entered under the name of a compiler, provided his name appears on the title-page. The designation *comp.* is put after the editor's name in the heading.

Title-page
    Modern Arabic short stories; Selected and
    Translated by Denys Johnson-Davies, with an
    introduction by Professor A. J. Arberry.
Main entry under *Johnson-Davies*

If no compiler's name appears on the title-page, main entry would be under the title of the collection. This rule is in accord with the minority decision at ICCP, the majority of delegates favouring entry under title. If a collection is published without a collective title, entry is under the heading appropriate to the first work listed on the title-page.

Title-page
    The Authorship of Wuthering Heights, by
    Irene Cooper Willis, and The Structure
    of Wuthering Heights by C. P. S.
Main entry under *Willis*

Serials (rule 6), *ie* publications issued in successive parts bearing numerical or chronological designations and intended to be continued indefinitely, are also examples of shared authorship, usually consisting of contributions by a number of persons, usually many more than three. Because they are intended to continue indefinitely, with the possibility of changes of editorship, they are known by their titles rather than by the names of their editors or compilers. Serials not issued by a corporate body, and not of personal authorship are to be entered under their titles.

Title-page
    Progress in Library Science, 1966; edited
    by Robert Collison . . .
Main entry under *title*

Serials issued by a corporate body are also to be entered under their titles. These would include periodicals, monographic series, a serially published bibliography, index, directory, almanac or yearbook, with added entry under the corporate body. But, if the title of the serial, not including the subtitle, includes the name or abbreviation of the name of the corporate body or consists solely of a generic term that requires the name of the body for adequate identification of the serial, it is entered under the name of the body.

Journal of Documentation—though published by Aslib would be entered under *title*.

A.L.A. Bulletin—would be entered under *American Library Association*.

Here again we have a simplification of the rules in previous codes, and also a rule based entirely on title-page information. The previous codes also based choice of entry on other considerations, such as whether the serial contained only the official transactions, etc of the corporate body, which is a condition very difficult to determine.

Serials issued by a personal author are to be entered under his name.

If the title of the serial, or the name of the corporate body under which entry is made, changes, entry is made for each title or name as it exists at the time of publication. This means that there will not be a complete list in one place in the catalogue of the complete holdings of any serial which changes its title. However, requests for serials are not usually for a long run, but for one number, and it is usually the title existing at the time of publication which is cited. Any library which wishes can compile such a complete list under a given title—earliest, latest or best-known.

WORKS OF AUTHORSHIP OF MIXED CHARACTER

This group comprises the type of multiple authorship where the contributions of the various authors are of different kinds—writing, adapting, translating, revising, editing, etc. With this group the basic concept of ' person or body primarily responsible '—as indicated by the relative importance of the different activities as such, the relative proportions of the work resulting from the different activities, and the emphasis given to each on the title-page—is the determinant of the heading. Rules follow for certain specified types of mixed authorship responsibility, but these are by no means exhaustive, and in other situations recourse must be had to the basic criterion of authorship—the person or body primarily responsible for the work. Reasons of space forbid treatment of each rule, and only those which present differences from existing practice, or are otherwise of interest, will be dealt with here.

Adapter or original author (rule 7): An adaptation or other rewriting of an original work in a different literary style (epitome, paraphrase, etc), or in a different literary form (dramatisation, novelisation, etc) is entered under the name of the person who did the adapting or the rewriting. If the adapter or rewriter is not known, entry is under the title. This varies from a similar rule in the 1908 code (rule 17) which entered such adaptations under the original author. It is worth emphasising that the new code follows the rule to its logical conclusion, and enters an anonymous adaptation under title. Thus anonymous adaptations of John Bunyan's *The pilgrim's progress* would each be entered under its own title, and not under Bunyan for main entry. This would appear to scatter material that would be better entered together.

Artist or author of text (rule 8): In the previous codes the entry of a work containing text and illustrative material was dependent upon a consideration of ' principal responsibility '. The position is generally the same in the present code, but a new category has been introduced, that of the collaborative work. When the work appears to be the result of collaboration between the author of the text and the artist it is to be entered under the name which appears first on the title-page. Added entry is made under the name not given main entry.

Title-page
> This is Belgium. 83 photographs by Cas
> Oorthuys. Text by K. Jonckheere.

Main entry under *Oorthuys*

In cases where an illustrated work is not the result of such collaboration, for example when an author comments on the previous work of an artist, or an artist illustrates a text previously written independently by an author, entry is under the person ' primarily responsible '.

Title-page
> Our Beautiful Homeland. Cambridge by Ruth
> Mellanby, with eight plates in colour from
> paintings by Leonard Squirrell ...

Main entry under *Mellanby*

Title-page
> W. G. Constable. Richard Wilson ...

Main entry under *Wilson* (Chief aim is to provide a corpus of Richard Wilson's subject pieces and land-scapes).

The principle of ' primary responsibility ' can account for rules 9, Biographer/critic or author; 10, Calligrapher or author; 11, Commentator or author; 12, Praeses or respondent in academic dissertations; 14, Reviser or original author; and 16, Writer or nominal author.

Reporter or person reported (rule 13): The report of an interview or discussion, or similar exchange between persons, is to be entered under the reporter, if he was a participant in the exchange, or if the report is mainly in his own words. If the reporter was not a participant, and the report is confined to the words of the person or persons interviewed, entry is under the principal participant, or the title, as the case may be, according to rule 3.

Title-page
> I killed to live. The Story of Eric Pleasants
> as told to Eddie Chapman.

Main entry under *Pleasants*

CORPORATE VERSUS PERSONAL AUTHORSHIP

One type of material which gives considerable difficulty in deciding the main heading comprises those publications which bear on their title-pages both the name of a personal and a corporate author. Whether to enter under the personal or the corporate name is often a difficult decision. The 1908 code gave very little guidance, the 1949 code somewhat more, but even it was still inadequate. Lack of guidance on this point caused cataloguers to define their own practices, and because of the very vague wording of the previous codes, the practice had evolved of basing the choice between a personal or a corporate heading on whether the person named on the title-page was or was not an official of the corporate body. If he was, entry was to be made under the name of the corporate body; if he was not, the entry was to be made under his name. In many cases the exact relationship between a person and a corporate body is not easy to assess, and, more importantly, the distinction is bibliographically irrelevant. The 1967 code applies the criterion of ' primary responsibility ', and would enter under the corporate body only such works as are by their nature the expression of the corporate thought and activity of the body, *ie* official records and reports, and statements, studies and other communications dealing with the policy, operations or management of the corporate body made by officers or other employees of the body. This is stated in rule 17A. For example, the *Annual report of the Librarian to Congress* would be entered under Library of Congress. Single reports made by officers or other employees of a corporate body that contain the results of scientific or scholarly research are excluded, unless written by more than three persons, none of whom is represented as the principal author.

In all other cases, according to rule 17B, entry is made under the appropriate heading, as if no corporate body were involved, *ie* under author or title. In all cases of doubt, the personal name is preferred to the corporate for main entry, with an added entry under the name of the corporate body, provided it does not act merely as publisher, when no added entry would be necessary.

 Title-page
  United Kingdom Atomic Energy Authority.
  Industrial Group. Nuclear Power and
  Reactor Engineering, Selected and
  annotated references, by J. C. Hartas,
  Library and Information Department,
  Research and Development Branch . . .
 Main entry under *Hartas*

Rule 18 deals with the choice for heading between a corporate body and one of its subordinate units. Generally the subordinate body is to be preferred as author, unless it merely acts as an information or publication agent for the parent body.

Title-page
   Illuminated Manuscripts in the Fitzwilliam
   Museum ... by Francis Wormald and Phyllis
   M. Gills ...
Main entry under *Fitzwilliam Museum*
Reference from University of Cambridge. *Fitzwilliam*
                                                          Museum
The form for the heading of a corporate body is determined in the
section of the code dealing with the form of name for corporate and
subordinate bodies, chapter 3.

RELATED WORKS
Rule 19 deals with related works. Some of the rules we have already
considered were concerned with one form of related work, *eg* adaptations, revisions, and translations. The related works covered by rule
19 are not merely different forms of the original work, as the former
are, but are those works which owe their existence or meaning to
previously existing works, such as continuations, supplements, indexes,
concordances, scenarios, extracts from serials, etc. Such works have
an independent existence of their own, and are usually to be entered
under their own authors, unless their titles are indistinctive, or are
dependent on the titles of other works, in which case they would be
entered under the heading for the original work. Thus concordances
are entered under their compilers, and not under the author concorded,
as in the British alternative rule in the 1908 code.
   Title-page
      A complete Word and Phrase Concordance to
      the Poems and Songs of Robert Burns ... Compiled
      and edited by J. B. Reid, M.A. ...
   Main entry under *Reid*
An exception to independent entry is made in the case of librettos
for particular musical compositions. These are to be entered under
the composer/title of the musical work. But, if the libretto has been
published as an independent literary work, it would be entered under
its own author. However, a footnote allows a libretto to be treated as
rule 19B, *ie* as an independent work to be entered under its own author.
The treatment of librettos in the 1967 code shows signs of indecision.
A much simpler solution would have been to treat a libretto and its
music in the same manner as a collaborative illustrated work (rule 8A).
There seems to be much in common between the two types of publication.
   The remainder of the rules in this section on 'entry' are special
rules covering special types of publication—laws, constitutions and
treaties, and certain religious publications. In some cases the two texts

differ. The student should examine the rules in this section for himself. It is perhaps a pity that the editors found it necessary to make rules for specific types of publications, as this practice is inconsistent with the main structure of the code, which is to give rules for particular types of *problem* rather than *publication*. In this section, also, certain form headings are advocated. Form headings had been eschewed by Lubetzky, but tolerated as a practical necessity by ICCP.

ADDED AND ANALYTICAL ENTRIES

In the foregoing pages, we have alluded frequently to the use of added entries, *ie* secondary entries. Added entries are needed to provide access to the record of a book or document in the catalogue under some characteristic other than that chosen for the main entry, for example, translator, editor, reviser, title, series, and, in a dictionary catalogue, subject. In smaller libraries, where each entry is written or typed separately, the detail on the added entries is reduced to a minimum, usually to the added entry heading, the title and name of author, edition, date, and class number. This distinction in the amount of information in main and added entries disappears with unit cataloguing, where each added entry is a replica of the main entry with appropriate added entry heading added at the top of the card. Unit entry is an essential economy when printed cards are used, such as those issued by the *British national bibliography*, or where a library duplicates its own cards. With unit cards, the only distinction between main and added entries, apart from the extra heading on added entries, is the ' tracings ' of the added entry headings added to the main entry card. Unit entries have the advantage that the user of the catalogue receives full information about the book he wants under whatever heading he may look for it. In the worked examples at the end of the book it is assumed that unit cataloguing is being used, and therefore the main entry is worked out in full detail, and only the headings for the added entries are indicated.

Rule 33 lists the circumstances in which added entries are to be used, apart from instructions with the individual rules:

1 For *collaborators*, when the main entry is under one of two or three authors. Added entries would be made under the other one or two. This rule also applies to editors and compilers (see also rule 3).

2 For an *openly named writer* (presumably one named on the title-page) when some other person or corporate body is given the main entry.

3 For *editors and compilers* named on the title-page, when the main entry is not under the name of a person. If the main entry is under a personal name, an added entry is only made under an editor when

he has added significant material, or the work has been revised many times by different editors.

4 *Translators.* Added entries are to be made under translators when the main entry is not under a personal name (*eg* anonymous works) if such an entry would give a useful approach to a publication. If the main entry is under a personal heading, an added entry is only made under a translator if the translation is in verse, or is important in its own right, or if the work has been translated into the same language by a number of different translators.

5 An *illustrator* would only receive an added entry if his contribution formed an important part of a work.

6 A *corporate body* named on a title-page would receive added entry provided its responsibility for a publication was more than that of publisher.

7 An added entry would also be made for any other person or body having some connection with a publication, and whose name might be used by an enquirer for retrieval purposes, for example, the person honoured in a festschrift.

8 If a person is only identified by initials, or by an abbreviation of his name, added entries should be made under the initials, both first and last if the initials represent the name of an author (such works being treated as anonymous).

9 If an author is identified only by a short descriptive phrase, which is not regarded as a pseudonym for entry purposes, an added entry would be made under the descriptive phrase. For example:

Main entry: A Voice from the ranks . . . by a Sergeant of the Royal Fusiliers.
Added entry: Sergeant of the Royal Fusiliers

10 Where an author describes himself as the author of another book he has written, an added entry would be made under the title quoted.

On title-page: . . . by the author of The martyrdom of an empress
Added entry: The Martyrdom of an empress, Author of

In all other cases, an added entry should be made under any other personal name which might provide an approach to a work, other than the subject approach.

Series: An added entry should be made under the title of a series for each catalogued work in the series. If the volumes in the series are numbered, the number should be added after the title of the series:

Practical library handbooks, no. 8
    Taylor, Margaret S.
        Fundamentals of practical cataloguing...

However, some discretion should be exercised in making series entries. General publishers' series, such as Nelson's 'Classics', do not warrant a series entry, but a subject series such as the 'New naturalist' series would warrant a series entry.

Titles: Added entry under title should be made for all titles that are distinctive and memorable. A title added entry must always be made for all anonymous works whose authors are known, and which would thus have entry under the author. The added entry under title is essential if the user of the catalogue is to find the entry. The code cites circumstances where added entry under title would *not* be made:

1 Common titles which would be meaningless without the personal or corporate author's name, *eg*

The Miscellaneous prose of Charles Lamb

Proceedings of the Royal Society

2 Long, involved, and non-distinctive titles, unless the main entry is under a corporate heading, or a heading which includes form subdivisions.

3 When the title consists solely of the name of a real person, *eg*
Kennedy, A. L.

Salisbury, 1830-1903: portrait of a statesman . . .

4 Works for which the cataloguer has composed a title.

5 In a *dictionary catalogue* under a title which would be identical with a subject heading. The subject entry would be preferred in a dictionary catalogue because it is linked to other subject headings by cross-references, while a title entry stands in isolation.

ANALYTICAL ENTRIES (RULE 156)

Analytical entries are entries for distinct parts of works which may be sought without reference to the work which contains them. Such entries must also contain a reference to the work which contains them, called the 'citation'. Analytical entries would certainly be made for the contents of each volume of a multi-volumed work, when the contents divided off into volumes. They would also be made for the authors and titles of all plays by different authors contained in collections of plays. Analytical subject entries would also be necessary in the subject catalogue. Most libraries have neither staff, time, nor money to practise analytical entries on a wide scale, relying on such published guides (in the UK) as the *British humanities index,* and the *British technology index,* etc. Analytical entries should not be made for material which one might reasonably expect to find in a larger work. For example, it would be ridiculous to make analytical entries for each of Shakespeare's plays contained in a collected edition of his works. But where a contents note has been added to an entry, always consider the need for analytical entries.

Form of analytical entries: An analytical entry consists of a description of the part analysed, followed by a short citation of the whole publication which contains the part analysed. The citation is normally enclosed in parentheses, and consists of the name of the author of the main work in the form used for the main entry heading, short title, edition, date, and the inclusive number of pages occupied by the part analysed, and the class-number for the main work.

Examples: Author and title analytical entries would be necessary for the *New English dramatists,* 9 on page 22.

Author analytical
Howarth, Donald
    A lily in little India (*in* New English
dramatists, 9. 1966, pp. 1-33).
ooo

Title analytical
A Lily in little India, by Donald Howarth (*in*
    New English dramatists, 9. 1966, pp. 1-33).
ooo

HEADINGS FOR PERSONS

This chapter deals with the problem of which name and which element of a name is to be used for the entry of personal authors. Rule 40 states the basic rule, that entry of a person is to be made under the name by which he is commonly identified, whether this be the real name, assumed name, nickname, title of nobility, or other appellation, for example:

Wodehouse, P. G.
Hunt, Leigh
Corbett, Jim
Lithgow, Mike

If an author is not commonly identified by one name or form of name in his works, the choice of name is to follow the undernoted order of preference:

1 Under the name by which he is identified in reference sources.

2 Under the name by which he is most frequently identified in his works.

3 Under the latest name he has used.

'Reference sources' are to be understood to include books and articles written about the person.

Authors of modern times are generally to be entered under their surnames, followed by their forenames or initials according to the title-page or the preference of the author. Use of the author's full name is no longer accepted cataloguing practice; initials representing forenames need only be expanded when confusion may arise between two or more authors having the same surname and initials (rule 43):

Mencken, H. L.

Lewis, C. S.

As a precaution, if two authors possess a common surname, the forenames should always be spelt out in full (rule 52), *eg*

Smith, Harry Alexander

Smith, Harry Arnold

If, after filling out the initials by full forenames, two or more authors' names are still identical, their dates of birth and death are to be added, if available.

Smith, Henry Allen, b. 1847

Smith, Henry Allen, 1907-

If dates are not available, any distinguishing term appearing on the title-page, or in reference sources should be added, *eg* academic degree:

Jones, Robert, *M.A.*

Similarly, when two or more noblemen have the same family name, personal names and title, and are represented in the catalogue, the ordinal number of the title should be included in the designation, otherwise it is not. The Roman numeral is only appended to the names of monarchs, if there have been two or more in the same country with the same name. The same applies to popes:

Charles I, *King of Great Britain*

Charles II, *King of Great Britain*

With a change of name, entry is made under the latest form of name or names, unless an earlier is better known.

Eden, Anthony, *Earl Avon*

x Avon, Anthony Eden, *Earl**

but

Amory, Derick Heathcoat, *Viscount* Amory

Pseudonymous works, ie works in which the author attempts to conceal or obscure his identity by using a false name, are to be entered under the pseudonym, provided the author uses one pseudonym consistently on the title-pages of all his works, with a reference from his real name (rule 42):

Henry, O.

x Porter, William Sidney

If, however, an author uses several pseudonyms in the course of his works, or his real name and one or more pseudonyms, entry is to be made under the form by which he is identified in reference sources.

---

* x signifies that a *see* reference would be made from the heading following it to the heading above.

In cases of doubt, the real name should be preferred. In this way the 1967 code attempts to maintain the ' literary unit ':

Tranter, Nigel
    x Tredgold, Nye

When an author uses more than one name, an exception may be made, and each work entered under the name used by the author on the title-page of each. This exception is suggested for popular libraries. References would be used to connect the different names used by the same author, thus still enabling the enquirer to find all the works written by the one person. Entry under each name has the advantage of directness. The *British national bibliography* enters under each pseudonym used by an author, as also does the British Museum. Notice, however, that the main rule does not mean entry under the real name in every case, but it does insist on entering all works by the one author under one name. The exception does not. The 1908 code was in favour of entry under the real name, whenever it was known.

Authors without surnames, or titles of nobility by which they are identified, are to be entered under the part of their names by which they are identified in reference sources, which will usually be the first part of the names they use. Any other name which they have acquired informally, such as a nickname, epithet or sobriquet, is to be added to the heading (rule 49):

William, of Ockham
Thomas, the Rhymer
Henry, the Navigator

If an appellation or pseudonym consisting of a word, phrase, or expression is always used to identify an author, and the name is obviously not the author's real name, the appellation or pseudonym should be entered in its direct form, and only be inverted when it contains a forename and a surname (rule 51):

Jim, Uncle   x Uncle Jim
Other, A. N.   x A. N. Other

Compound surnames are entered under the first part, with a reference from the second part (rule 46):

Kahn-Freund, Otto
    x Freund, Otto Kahn-
Cervantes Saavedra, Miguel de

Compound or hyphenated surnames are always to be entered under the part preceding the hyphen, even if the author does not regularly use the hyphenated form. Caution, however, should be exercised with popular authors commonly known by a name which appears to be a compound, but is not in reality:

Doyle, *Sir* Arthur Conan
    x Conan Doyle, *Sir* Arthur

Maugham, William Somerset

 x Somerset Maugham, William

If a personal name is found in different language forms, the general ruling is to enter it under the form found in reference sources.

Surnames with prefixes (rule 46): Surnames which include separately written prefixes should be entered under the form used in reference sources in the author's language. English authors are to be entered under the prefix:

Dos Passos, John

De Morgan, Charles

Ap Williams, Hugh

McDonald, Hector

In all cases, references would be made from the part following the prefix. The rules for names with prefixes in other languages have as their aim entry under the element by which an author would be known in his own language. The usages of the major languages are set out in detail in rules 46E/F, and the student is referred to the rulings given there. In general, if the prefix is not an article or preposition or a combination of the two, entry is under the prefix.

Noblemen are entered under their titles, whenever this is the name by which they are best known, and reference is made from their family names. The heading should consist of three elements: 1 family name; 2 forename(s); 3 title. If, as is often the case, the family name and the title are the same, entry under the family name is to be preferred, but the title would still be included in the heading:

Melbourne, William Lamb, *Viscount*

 x Lamb, William, Viscount Melbourne

Balfour, Arthur James, *Earl Balfour*

The exact title must be used, and not the commonly used form of address 'Lord'. British titles of honour—Sir, Dame, Lord, Lady, Honourable, etc are to precede the forenames in the heading:

Scott, *Sir* Walter, *Bart*

Macmillan, *Lady* Dorothy

Churchill, *Lord* Randolph

The wife of a nobleman has the title corresponding to that of her husband, and the wife of a baronet or knight has the title 'Lady' suffixed to the heading. As Cutter says in his *Rules*, 'Women who marry have everything to gain and nothing to lose so far as titles are concerned'. If a woman has a courtesy title by right of her birth, she keeps it, even if she marries a commoner, as Lady Dorothy Macmillan given above. If she is a commoner, and marries a member of the nobility or a knight or a baronet, she acquires the appropriate title; in the last two cases the title 'Lady':

Bradford, Sarah Sheridan, *Lady*

A *King or a monarch* should be entered under his forename with his title designation added in English, which is also to include the name of the state or people governed:

Louis XIV, *King of France*

Epithets usually associated with the name of a monarch are not included in the heading. They are always ignored in filing:

Henry, *King of Castille*
    x Henry the Sickly

As stated earlier, numerals are only used after the names of sovereigns, etc if more than one with the same name has ruled over the same territory or peoples:

John, *King of Poland*

Forenames should also be used for entering Christian saints, with the designation *Saint* added. If, however, the person in question was also an emperor, king, or pope, he should be entered as such with a reference from his name as saint:

Louis IX, *King of France*
    x Louis IX, *Saint, King of France*

Popes should be entered under their pontifical names, with the designation added in English:

John XXII, *Pope*

After the names of bishops, cardinals, and other church dignitaries should be added their titles in English, and if the person has more than one title, the suffix should be the highest rank. Persons with the same name, rank, and see are distinguished by Roman numerals as found in reference sources:

Augustine, *Saint, Abp. of Canterbury*
Augustine, *Saint, Bp. of Hippo*
Newman, John Henry, *Cardinal*

Other persons in religion should be entered under the form of name which they use regularly. In the case of Christian priests, the initials of the order are included only if regularly used by the person.

HEADINGS FOR CORPORATE BODIES

The rules for entering corporate bodies were among the most unsatisfactory rules in both the 1908 and 1949 codes. Corporate bodies suffer more than personal authors from a lack of distinctness in their names. For this reason the two earlier codes recognised basically three types of corporate body: governments, societies, and institutions. The distinction between the latter two was that societies were assumed to be corporate bodies which generally possessed distinctive names, which could be used as they stood for entry, while the names of institutions were not generally so distinctive, and were not adequate for entry purposes. Thus, the general rule for institutions was to enter them under the name of the place where they were located. The first group, governments, were to be entered under the name of the area over which they exercised jurisdiction. The distinction between societies and institutions was never satisfactory, for various reasons. In the first place the distinction had no basis in reality. Quite a number of institutions do have distinctive names, *eg*

British Museum

Johns Hopkins University

While many societies do not have distinctive names, *eg*

Royal Society

The attempt was also made in the previous codes to justify the distinction between the two types of corporate body in terms of their administrative structures. The specifications given under the two types of body indicated that societies were corporate bodies which could operate anywhere, while institutions were bodies which needed buildings, plant, and equipment to operate successfully, and thus tended to become identified with a particular place. Such a distinction is, however, completely irrelevant to the cataloguing problem presented by the names of corporate bodies as printed on the title-pages of books.

The 1967 code avoids many of these difficulties by recognising only two types of corporate body—government bodies, which are to be entered under the name of the area over which they exercise jurisdiction, and other corporate bodies, which are to be entered under their names as they stand. The basic rule is to enter such bodies under their names, whatever their administrative structure, unless their names obviously imply subordination to some higher body:

Library Association

University of Glasgow

Edinburgh Chamber of Commerce

The North American text incorporates some modifications to this general rule for certain specified types of corporate body, but these we shall examine later.

The remainder of the rules in this section deal with modifications and amplifications to this basic rule of entry under name. Only the more important modifications and amplifications can be dealt with in a textbook of this size, and the student is advised to study the detailed rules for himself.

Change of name of corporate body: The first complication with corporate bodies as authors, especially if they are all to be entered under their names as they stand, is that they do not always consistently use the same name or form of name on the title-pages of their publications. Corporate bodies often change their names, a change which may or may not reflect a change in the functions, purposes, or administrative structure of the bodies themselves. Often the full name of a corporate body is seldom used. The codes of 1908 and 1949 advocated the use of the full corporate names of bodies, while the 1967 code, in rule 61, prefers to follow the form of name as given on the publications of which it is an author, publisher, or sponsor, even if this form should differ from that given in reference courses. If variant forms are to be found in a corporate body's own publications, the form as it appears in formal presentations at the head of the title, in the imprint, or in formal author statements is to be preferred to a form found in the running text or in titles (rule 62), *eg*

British Association
   x British Association for the Advancement of Science
If variant forms are found in formal presentations, the brief form, consisting of initials or syllables of the name, is to be preferred to the full official form, *eg*

Unesco
   x United Nations Educational Scientific and Cultural Organization
   x U.N.E.S.C.O.
Aslib
   x Association of Special Libraries and Information Bureaux
Similarly, when a body is known by a conventional form of name in reference sources in its own language, the conventional form of name is to be preferred to the official form.

If the name appears in different languages, the form in the official language is to be preferred, and always the form in English, if it is one of the official languages:

South African Library Association
   x Suid-Afrikaanse Biblioteekvereeniging
The same will apply if the corporate body is international in scope, having official names in more than one language.

Because corporate bodies are now to be entered under their names as they stand, the addition of a country or place name may have to be given *after* the name of the body to distinguish two or more bodies in different countries or places with otherwise identical names (rule 65B):

Liberal Party (Gt. Brit.)
Liberal Party (Canada)
Initial articles may be omitted from the name of a corporate body in the heading, provided it is not required for reasons of clarity or grammar:

Library Association (not The Library Association).
Similarly, adjectives denoting royal privilege may be omitted from the beginning of a name in any European language, except English,

or if the omission may reduce the name to a common word or phrase:
Royal Automobile Club

Corporate bodies, as we have already noted, often change their names. There was no rule in the 1908 code to cover this contingency. The case of change of name with personal authors is not exactly parallel. A personal author who changes his name is still the same person, but the same does not necessarily hold when a corporate body changes its name, as we have already stated. For this reason rule 68 enters the publications of a corporate body which changes its name under each name existing at the time of publication. Cross references are to be used to link the various names:

Glasgow and West of Scotland Commercial College
became
Scottish College of Commerce
which became
University of Strathclyde. *Scottish College*
' See also ' references would be used to link the names.

SUBORDINATE CORPORATE BODIES

Corporate bodies which are subordinate to larger organisations pose a problem. Two lines of approach can be adopted: 1 To enter under the parent body, and so preserve the administrative hierarchy of the bodies concerned; 2 use the name of the subordinate body directly as the heading, if the name of the subordinate body is sufficiently distinctive to be used on its own. The 1908 and 1949 codes were inconsistent in that they applied the first solution to subordinate institutions, and the second to subordinate societies. Thus the Bodleian Library was always subordinated in the heading to the University of Oxford, while the Scottish Library Association was entered under its own name, and not as a branch of the Library Association.

The 1967 code is more consistent and applies the criterion of self-sufficiency of name to all types of subordinate body. This is achieved by rules 69 and 70, *eg*

Bodleian Library
    x University of Oxford. *Bodleian Library*
Andersonian Library
    x University of Strathclyde. *Andersonian Library*

However, those subordinate bodies whose names obviously imply subordination, and are not self-sufficient in themselves are to be entered under the name of the parent body. The whole hierarchy of subordination need not be given; intervening elements in the hierarchy that are not essential to clarify the function of the subordinate body are to be omitted from the heading, *eg*

44

United Kingdom Atomic Energy Authority. *Industrial Group. Library and Information Department*
  x United Kingdom Atomic Energy Authority. *Industrial Group. Research and Development Branch. Library and Information Department*

Consistent with the practice of the 1967 code of choosing for entry the name by which a corporate body is identified, the English form of name of the area over which a government exercises jurisdiction is preferred to the foreign, and in the conventional rather than the full official form, *eg*

France
  x République française
Edinburgh
  x County of the city of Edinburgh

As modern governmental activity enters many fields apart from its basic legislative, judicial and executive functions, the problem often arises as to whether certain departments of government and boards and agencies controlled by government should be entered under the name of the government or the name of the board or agency. This was a problem not faced at all by the 1908 code, largely because governmental control was not then so extensive as now.

The present code generally restricts entry under the names of governments to those bodies exercising the basic legislative, judicial or executive functions of government. These would be entered as subheadings under the name of the country, etc:

GREAT BRITAIN. *Department of Education and Science*
UNITED STATES. *Department of the Interior*

In all other cases entry is made under the name of the body. Other bodies and organisations, created and controlled by a government, are to be entered under their own names, if they belong to one of the seven categories of such bodies listed in rule 78A. These are to include, amongst others, organisations engaged in commercial, cultural, or scientific activities, *eg*

National Engineering Laboratory, *East Kilbride*
Forest Products Research Laboratory
Institutions and installations:
  British Museum
  Kielder National Forest Park
Authorities and trusts for the operation of utilities and industries:
  North of Scotland Hydro Electric Board
  Scottish Gas Board
Established churches:
  Church of Scotland
  Church of England

Rule 78B states that if a government body is not one of the types listed in the seven categories of rule 78A, or if there is doubt as to whether it is one of these categories, entry is under the name of the government (see worked examples, nos 24 and 25).

Subordinate agencies of government are treated similarly to other subordinate bodies, being entered directly under the name of the government, if the name of the subordinate body or unit is not likely to be used by another body in the same jurisdiction:

UNITED STATES. *Bureau of the Census*
   x UNITED STATES. *Department of Commerce. Bureau of the Census*

The official publications of chiefs of state, sovereigns, presidents, governors, etc. are to be entered under the title of their office in English (rule 80A), followed by the inclusive years of the reign or incumbency, *eg*

GREAT BRITAIN. *Sovereign, 1910-1936 (George V)*

The private communications of such persons—letters, speeches, etc would be entered under the name of the person:

GEORGE V, *King of Great Britain, 1865-1936*

Conferences, congresses, meetings, etc (rules 87-91) are best regarded as temporary corporate bodies, and the official accounts of their proceedings, transactions, etc are entered under the name of the conference or meeting, followed by one or more of the following elements—number, place, date (rule 69C). This rule does not apply to meetings, councils, or conventions of an organisation representing its membership; such publications would be entered under the name of the corporate body:

Symposium on the Pathology of Parasitic Diseases. *4th. London. 1965*

but

Library Association. Proceedings of the public libraries conference
. . .

A conference or congress is regarded as having a name, if the phrase referring to it is in the form of a specific appellation, rather than that of a general description (see the footnote to rule 87). If a meeting lacks such a name, its publications would be treated according to the general rules for entry, *ie* under principal author, title, or editor, *eg*

BOAZ, Martha, *ed.*
   Modern trends in documentation: proceedings of a symposium held at the University of California, April, 1958 . . .

Rules 92 to 96 deal with the names of religious bodies and organisations, and are omitted here for reasons of space.

The North American text contains two rules (rules 98 and 99) which constitute exceptions to entry of corporate bodies under their names for certain types of body with particular forms of name They are not repeated in the British text. The exceptions are largely the result of pressure from the Library of Congress and the larger research libraries in the United States to avoid the changes in headings in their catalogues, had the original proposals been put into effect. The exceptions include local churches, educational institutions, libraries, galleries, museums, agricultural experiment stations, airports, botanical and zoological gardens and hospitals. If the names of any of these bodies consist solely of a common word or phrase, followed by the name of the municipality or other wider jurisdiction less than the national level in which it is located, or such a word or phrase qualified by an adjective indicating one of these jurisdictions by its type, entry is under the jurisdiction named or implied, followed by the name of the body, *eg*

    LONDON. University
    MANCHESTER. Public library

Although the types of corporate body and the forms of name are strictly defined, the result is that entries for many bodies which would have been classified as ' institutions ' by the previous codes remain under the name of the place where the body is located.

UNIFORM TITLES

This section of the 1967 code (chapter 4) introduces a new concept to users of the 1908 code, the option of introducing ' uniform titles '. It stems from the need to enter all editions, versions, and translations of a work in one place in the catalogue. Lubetzky used the phrase ' bibliographic unit ' to describe the assemblage of all texts of the one work in one place in the catalogue, no matter how different versions of the work are named on their title-pages. The 1908 code took little cognisance of the bibliographic unit as such. In only two rules, those for the *Bible*, and for anonymous ' classics ', was entry preferred under a uniform title, to bring all versions of what is basically the same text together. The concept of the bibliographic unit emphasises the point that we are primarily interested in the *work*, rather than its physical presentation in any particular *book*.

The basic rule (rule 100) is to enter under *one* title works which are published in various editions and translations with varying titles. In title entries the heading should consist of the uniform title, and with entries under authors, the uniform title (within square brackets) should precede the title given on the title-page of the book being catalogued. The one exception is for a revision of an original work appearing under a different title. The title of each edition should be used, with the earlier or later title noted on each entry.

Having decided on the need for uniform titles, the important question is which title to use. Modern works written after 1500 are to be entered under the title of the *original* edition (rule 101A):

Spring, Howard

    [O Absalom] My son, My son

Spring, Howard

    My son, my son

    See his O Absalom

Introductory phrases which are not part of the title proper, such as 'Here beginneth the tale of . . .', and in the case of anonymous works, initial articles, are omitted wherever possible. An exception may be made in favour of entry under a later title, when it is shorter, and in modern spelling, when this has become better known in reference sources, and through use in later editions:

Dickens, Charles

    [David Copperfield]. The personal history of David Copperfield . . .

If a work is published simultaneously in the same language in different countries, with different titles, the uniform title is to be that of the edition published in the country where the library is situated.

The uniform title for works written before 1500 is generally to be that in the original language by which the work has become identified in reference sources, *eg*

Lucretius Carus, Titus

    [De rerum natura] On the nature of things.

Translations are to be entered under their titles in the language of the the original, with the name of the language into which they have been translated added after the original title (rule 105):

Stendhal

    [La chartreuse de Parme. English]

    The charterhouse of Parma . . .

  Added entry under title

    La Chartreuse de Parme

      The Charterhouse of Parma, by Stendhal . . .

To enter all translations under their original titles may be convenient in a library with a large collection of foreign literature, but in a popular library where foreign literature is mainly in translation into English, this rule would not be very convenient. The latter type of library may prefer to build the 'bibliographic unit' on the translated title. The advantage of using the original title is that a work may have been translated more than once into English, with different English titles for each translation. In a larger, more academic library it is likely that the original will be acquired before the translation, but even in this type of library trouble may be experienced with titles in non-Roman alphabets, for example, Russian. In a technical library even a transliteration into English would not be particularly helpful, when such a work will be universally known in this country by its translated title.

The device of the uniform title is essential for collected and selected editions of an author's works, different versions of which could have such titles as ' Collected works ', ' Complete works ', ' Works ', ' Selections ', etc. To catalogue these according to any particular title found on each title-page would be to scatter material which should be kept together in the catalogue. In the absence of any provision for a uniform title in the 1908 code, libraries usually catalogued from each title-page and relied on guide cards to arrange the entries together. Now, with the use of uniform titles, the heading or title itself will arrange the entry in the correct place.

Rule 107 advises the use of the uniform title ' Works ' for all collected editions of an author's works, no matter what title is used on the title-pages of the different editions. It is usual to subarrange by editor or date, though this is not stated in the 1967 code, *eg*

Burns, Robert

[Works] The complete poems and letters of Robert Burns . . .

The formal title ' Selected works ' is to be used for partial collections, if an author has written in various literary forms, or for partial collections of his works, if he has written in a single literary form:

Masefield, John

[Selected works] The narrative poems of John Masefield . . .

The uniform title ' Selections ' is to be used for extracts, quotations, etc from an author's works, *eg*

Shakespeare, William

[Selections] Gems from Shakespeare's plays and sonnets . . .

Detailed rules for uniform title entry for the Bible and similar sacred texts and liturgical works are also given in rules 108 to 119.

REFERENCES

The rules in the preceding chapters have dealt with the problem of under which name or part of a name a personal or corporate author should be entered. The alternative names or methods of citing a name must be catered for. It would be totally uneconomic to make added entries under the alternative names or forms of name, and as a general rule a personal author is entered in the catalogue under only one name or form of name. References (chapter 5) are made from alternative names or forms of name. A reference is a direction from one heading to another. There are two main types of reference: 1 a *See* reference from a heading under which no entries are made to an alternative heading which is used for entry; 2 a *See also* reference from one heading to another related heading, under both of which entries are to be found. *See also* references are most commonly used between subject headings in a dictionary catalogue, but they may also occasionally be used in an author/title catalogue as well. It should also be remembered that references are needed not only for names used as headings for main entries, but also when used as added entries.

The basic rule (rule 120) is that whenever a name of a person or corporate body, or the title of a work, may be known under a form other than that used for the heading or the uniform title, a reference should be made from the form not used to that used.

References are required from different names of persons and corporate bodies, *eg*

Ephesian
  See Bechhofer, Carl Eric
Ordo Sancti Benedicti
  See Benedictines

and from different forms of name:

Hunt, John Henry Leigh
  See Hunt, Leigh
American Red Cross
  See American National Red Cross

from different entry elements in the case of personal names:

Aitken, William Maxwell, *Baron Beaverbrook*
  See Beaverbrook, William Maxwell Aitken, *Baron*

from different forms of entry:

Great Britain. *National Physical Laboratory, Teddington*
  See National Physical Laboratory, *Teddington*

Explanatory references are used when more detailed guidance than can be given in a short reference is required:

Golon, Serge
  For works of this author written in collaboration with Anne Golon, *see under* Golon, Sergeanne.

When a uniform title is in use references must obviously be made from the variant titles under which the work has been published or cited in reference sources.

References may also be used in place of added entries, where their use would obviate the need for a large number of added entries. For example, most general libraries have many copies of *Robinson Crusoe*. Rather than make a title added entry for every version in the library, a reference to the author for full details of the various editions in the library will save a lot of space.

Robinson Crusoe
Daniel Defoe
  Editions of this work will be found under the author's name.

FACSIMILE TITLE PAGES

ECOLOGY
OF
PARASITES

by

N. A. CROLL, B.Sc., Ph.D., A.R.C.S.

Department of Zoology and Applied Entomology
Imperial College of Science and Technology, London

HEINEMANN EDUCATIONAL
BOOKS LTD : LONDON

Book is 7½ inches high. It has 8 unnumbered pages, followed by pages numbered 1 to 136 in Arabic. There are 35 diagrams, 7 plates, 2 maps and three pages of tables. On the verso of the title-page appears © N. A. Croll/ First published 1966.

THE

QUEEN'S QUAIR

OR

The Six Years' Tragedy

BY

MAURICE HEWLETT

'Improbus ille puer, crudelis tu quoque Mater'

London
MACMILLAN AND CO., Limited
NEW YORK : THE MACMILLAN COMPANY
1904

Book is 7½ inches high, and has 6 unnumbered pages, followed by pages vii and viii, one unnumbered page, then pages 2 & 3 numbered in Arabic, one unnumbered, page 5 numbered in Arabic, one unnumbered page, followed by pages 7 to 509 numbered in Arabic, then one unnumbered, followed by 18 pages of advertisements.

SAMUEL BUTLER'S NOTEBOOKS

Selections edited by

GEOFFREY KEYNES and BRIAN HILL

JONATHAN CAPE
THIRTY BEDFORD SQUARE
LONDON

Book is 7.7 inches high. There are 4 unnumbered pages, followed by pages numbered 5 to 327 in Arabic. On the verso of the title-page there appears: 'Samuel Butler's notebooks 1951/ Reprinted 1952.' Samuel Butler was born in 1835 and died in 1902.

REPRODUCTION

OF

SOUND

by Edgar Villchur

ACOUSTIC RESEARCH, INC., *Cambridge, Massachusetts*

DOVER PUBLICATIONS, INC., *New York*

Book is $8\frac{1}{2}$ inches high, and has 4 unnumbered pages, followed by pages 1 to 92 numbered in Arabic. There are numerous illustrations. On the verso of the title-page appears: ' © 1962 by Acoustic Research Inc./ © 1965 by Dover Publications Inc.' ' This Dover Edition first published in 1965, is a revised and enlarged republication of the work first published by Acoustic Research Inc. . . . in 1962.'

ENGLISH LITERATURE
IN THE
SIXTEENTH CENTURY
EXCLUDING DRAMA

BY

C. S. LEWIS
FELLOW OF MAGDALEN COLLEGE, OXFORD

The Completion of
THE CLARK LECTURES
Trinity College, Cambridge
1944

OXFORD
AT THE CLARENDON PRESS

Book is 8½ inches high. There are 5 unnumbered pages, followed by page 6 numbered in Roman, 3 unnumbered pages, then pages 2 to 696 numbered in Arabic. On verso of the title-page: ' First published 1954. Reprinted 1959, 1962.' On the page facing the title-page there appears: ' The Oxford History of English Literature, edited by F. P. Wilson and Bonamy Dobrée. No. III.'

EXAMPLE NO 6

The Image
of the Federal Service

FRANKLIN P. KILPATRICK
MILTON C. CUMMINGS, JR.
M. KENT JENNINGS

THE BROOKINGS INSTITUTION
WASHINGTON, D.C.

Book is 9 inches high, and has 8 unnumbered pages, followed by pages numbered ix to xvii, one page unnumbered, and pages numbered 1 to 301 in Arabic. On verso of title-page: © 1964, published Jan. 1964.

CYTOGENETICS

Carl P. Swanson
Timothy Merz
William J. Young

The Johns Hopkins University

PRENTICE-HALL, INC.   Englewood Cliffs, New Jersey

Book is 8.9 inches high, and has 5 unnumbered pages, followed by pages 6 to 12 numbered in Roman, and 1 to 194 numbered in Arabic. There are numerous illustrations, and the frontispiece is a facsimile. There is a bibliography at the end of each chapter.

Persistence and Change:

*Bennington College and
Its Students
After Twenty-five Years*

THEODORE M. NEWCOMB

The University of Michigan

KATHRYN E. KOENIG

York University

RICHARD FLACKS

The University of Chicago

DONALD P. WARWICK

The University of Michigan

JOHN WILEY & SONS, INC.   NEW YORK   LONDON   SYDNEY

Book is 9 inches high, and has 4 unnumbered pages, followed by pages 5 to 8 numbered in Roman, 4 pages unnumbered, and pages 3 to 292 numbered in Arabic. Book was published in 1967.

SHAKESPEARE
IN MUSIC

Essays by

JOHN STEVENS
CHARLES CUDWORTH
WINTON DEAN
ROGER FISKE

*

With a Catalogue of Musical Works

*

EDITED BY

PHYLLIS HARTNOLL

LONDON
MACMILLAN & CO LTD
NEW YORK · ST MARTIN'S PRESS
1964

Book is 8.4 inches high. There are 4 unnumbered pages, followed by pages 5 to 9 numbered in Roman, 3 unnumbered, followed by pages numbered 3 to 333.

The separate essays are as follows:—John Stevens. Shakespeare and the music of the Elizabethan stage, pp. 3 to 48; Charles Cudworth. Song and part-song settings of Shakespeare's lyrics, 1660-1960, pp. 51 to 87; Winton Dean. Shakespeare and the opera, pp. 89-175; Roger Fiske. Shakespeare in the concert hall, pp. 177 to 241; Catalogue of Musical works based on the plays and poetry of Shakespeare; compiled by Winton Dean, Dorothy Moore, and Phyllis Hartnoll, pp. 243 to 290.

CHEMICAL KINETICS

by

A. F. TROTMAN-DICKENSON

Professor of Chemistry
University College of Wales, Aberystwyth

SURFACE AND
COLLOID CHEMISTRY

by

G. D. PARFITT

Lecturer in Physical Chemistry
University of Nottingham

PERGAMON PRESS

OXFORD · LONDON · EDINBURGH · NEW YORK
TORONTO · PARIS · FRANKFURT

Book is 7.7 inches high. There are 4 unnumbered pages, followed by page 5 numbered in Roman, 1 unnumbered, page 7 in Roman, 1 unnumbered, pages numbered ix to x, 2 unnumbered, followed by pages numbered 3 to 71, 3 unnumbered, followed by pages numbered 75 to 170. There are illustrations and tables, and a plate on p. 127. There is also a bibliography on p. 164. On half-title-page appears: ' Commonwealth and International Library, Intermediate Chemistry Division; edited by J. E. Spice, 1966 '.

PÆDAGOGICA
EVROPÆA

The European Yearbook of Educational Research

Revue annuelle des études et recherches pédagogiques européennes

Europäisches Jahrbuch für pädagogische Forschung

PUBLISHED WITH THE SUPPORT OF THE
Council for Cultural Cooperation of The Council of Europe

EDITEE AVEC LE CONCOURS DU
Conseil de la Coopération Culturelle du Conseil de l'Europe

VERÖFFENTLICHT MIT UNTERSTÜTZUNG DES
Rates für kulturelle Zusammenarbeit des Europarates

1965
FIRST VOLUME / PREMIER VOLUME
ERSTER BAND

AGON ELSEVIER
AMSTERDAM AND BRUSSELS
GEORG WESTERMANN VERLAG
BRAUNSCHWEIG

Book is 9½ inches high, and has 4 unnumbered pages, followed by pages numbered v to xii, followed by pages numbered 1 to 284.

BIBLIOGRAPHY AND FOOTNOTES

A Style Manual
for College and University Students

By PEYTON HURT

❧

REVISED AND ENLARGED BY

MARY L. HURT RICHMOND

CUSTODIAN, CHAPIN LIBRARY
WILLIAMS COLLEGE

UNIVERSITY OF CALIFORNIA PRESS
BERKELEY AND LOS ANGELES
1963.

Book has 6 unnumbered pages, followed by pages numbered vii to xii, and 1 to 167. It is 8 inches high. On the verso of the title-page appears: © 1949. 5th printing 1963. A list of references is given on pages 155 and 156.

The Best of Beachcomber

SELECTED AND INTRODUCED BY
MICHAEL FRAYN

PENGUIN BOOKS

Book is 7 inches high. There are 5 unnumbered pages, then pages numbered 6 to 8, 1 unnumbered, and pages numbered 10 to 256. On verso of title-page: ' First published 1963 by Heinemann/ Published by Penguin 1966.' Penguin Books are published at Harmondsworth, Middlesex. ' Beachcomber ' is the pseudonym of J. B. Morton.

Word Index
to James Joyce's
Portrait of the Artist

Leslie Hancock

Southern Illinois University Press, *Carbondale and Edwardsville*

Feffer & Simons, Inc., *London and Amsterdam*

Book is 9 inches high, and there are 4 unnumbered pages, followed by pages numbered v to ix, 5 unnumbered pages, and pages numbered 3 to 145. On the verso of the title-page appears: © 1967.

T.L.S. 1962

Essays and Reviews from
The Times Literary Supplement

London
OXFORD UNIVERSITY PRESS
NEW YORK · TORONTO
1963

Book is 8½ inches high. There are 4 unnumbered pages, followed by pages 5 to 8 numbered in Roman, and pages 1 to 240 numbered in Arabic.

August Strindberg

The Son of a Servant
The Story of the Evolution of a Human Being
1849–67

Newly translated, with an Introduction and Notes,
by Evert Sprinchorn

Jonathan Cape
Thirty Bedford Square
London

Book is 7.7 inches high, there are 6 unnumbered pages followed by
pages numbered 7 to 223. On the verso of the title-page: ' This translation first published in Great Britain 1967/ Introduction, translation
and notes © 1966 by Evert Sprinchorn.' The original Swedish title
is: ' Tjanslekvinnans son '.

CHEMISTRY AND BIOLOGY LABORATORIES

DESIGN — CONSTRUCTION — EQUIPMENT

by

WERNER SCHRAMM

Second revised and supplemented
German edition with illustrations

Translation Editor
J. M. LEYTHAM

Translator
MRS. M. JANSEN

PERGAMON PRESS
OXFORD · LONDON · EDINBURGH · NEW YORK
PARIS · FRANKFURT

Book is 11 inches high. There are 16 pages of advertisements, followed by 4 unnumbered pages, pages numbered v to ix, 1 unnumbered, and pages numbered 1 to 255. There is a bibliography on pp. 250 to 255, and there are 787 figures in the text. On verso of title-page: © 1960. First English Edition 1965. The original German edition had the title: ' Chemische und Biologische Laboratorien '.

SCIENCE MUSEUM

A Directory and Nomenclature of the First Aeroplanes 1809 to 1909

by

CHARLES H. GIBBS-SMITH
M.A., F.M.A., Honorary Companion R.Ae.S.

LONDON

HER MAJESTY'S STATIONERY OFFICE

1966

Book is 9¾ inches high. There are 4 unnumbered pages, followed by p. 5 numbered in Roman, 1 unnumbered page, and pages 8 to 11 numbered in Roman, 3 unnumbered pages, and pages numbered 3 to 120 numbered in Arabic. There are tables throughout the text.

Copyright Law

OF THE

UNITED STATES OF AMERICA

Bulletin No. 14

(Revised to Jan. 1, 1967)

COPYRIGHT OFFICE

THE LIBRARY OF CONGRESS

Washington, D.C.   20540

1967

Book is 9 inches high, and there are 4 pages numbered in Roman, followed by 87 numbered in Arabic.

new rules

for

an old game

Edited by
Thelma E. Allen
Daryl Ann Dickman

Proceedings of a workshop
on the 1967 Anglo-American
cataloguing code
held by the School of Librarianship
The University of British Columbia
April 13 and 14, 1967

b LONDON

CLIVE BINGLEY
1968

Book is 9 inches high, and has 12 unnumbered pages, followed by pages numbered 13 to 175. On verso of title-page: First published 1967 by the University of British Columbia. There is a bibliography on pages 161-165.

Frank Pakenham
Earl of Longford

FIVE LIVES

HUTCHINSON OF LONDON

Book is 8.2 inches high, and has 8 unnumbered pages, followed by pages numbered from 9 to 279 in Arabic. The frontispiece is a portrait. On verso of title-page appears : © 1964.

MINISTRY OF DEFENCE

The Admiralty Hydrographic Service 1795-1919

VICE-ADMIRAL SIR ARCHIBALD DAY
K.B.E. C.B. D.S.O.
Formerly Hydrographer of the Navy

LONDON
HER MAJESTY'S STATIONERY OFFICE
1967

Book is 9½ inches high. It has 5 unnumbered pages, followed by pages numbered 6 to 378 in Arabic. There is one facsimile, coloured maps, and plates in the form of folding charts. On the verso of the title-page appears: Continuation of Dawson's Memoirs of Hydrography, Parts I & II, completed in 1885. Dawson's full name is: L. S. Dawson.

DEPARTMENT OF
SCIENTIFIC AND INDUSTRIAL RESEARCH

ROAD RESEARCH LABORATORY

Road Research Technical Paper No. 63

50-Point Traffic Census— the First 5 Years

By

J. C. TANNER, M.A., F.S.S.,

and

J. R. SCOTT, B.Sc., A.Inst.P., F.S.S.

LONDON

HER MAJESTY'S STATIONERY OFFICE

1962

Pamphlet is 9½ inches high, and has 2 unnumbered pages, page 3 numbered in Roman, 2 unnumbered pages, and page 6 numbered in Roman, followed by pages 1 to 38 numbered in Arabic. There are also tables and diagrams.

SCOTTISH HOME AND HEALTH DEPARTMENT

SCOTTISH HEALTH SERVICES COUNCIL

Administrative Practice
of Hospital Boards
in Scotland

REPORT BY A COMMITTEE
OF THE SCOTTISH HEALTH SERVICES
COUNCIL

EDINBURGH
HER MAJESTY'S STATIONERY OFFICE
1966

Pamphlet has 1 unnumbered page, pages 2 to 109 numbered in Arabic, 9½ inches high, with tables. Chairman is W. M. Farquharson-Lang.

Cabinet Office

THE
TORREY
CANYON

*Report of the Committee of Scientists on the
Scientific and Technological Aspects of the
Torrey Canyon Disaster*

London: Her Majesty's Stationery Office 1967

Pamphlet is 9½ inches high, has 8 pages numbered in Roman, and 47
in Arabic; some plates. Chairman is Sir Solly Zuckerman.

WORKED EXAMPLES

Main entry

CROLL, N. A.
   Ecology of parasites ... London: Heinemann,
1966.
   [8], 136p., 7 plates; 35 illus., maps.   20cm.
                              000

COMMENT
Straightforward example of single personal authorship covered by rule
1. The degrees, etc of an author are omitted, and the omission indicated
by three dots (...). The author's name has not been repeated in the
title transcript because it does not differ from the form appearing in
the heading. Again, the omission is indicated by three dots. In the
collation, the 8 unnumbered pages are not accounted for by the
existing pagination and would have to be included in square brackets.
The term ' illus.' is used to cover diagrams. Tables are regarded as
textual matter and ignored in the statement of the illustrations (see
rule 143D1b). Title entry would not be required, as this approach
would be adequately covered by the subject entry.

EXAMPLE NO 2

Main entry

HEWLETT, Maurice
   The queen's quair; or, The six years' tragedy ...
London, New York: Macmillan, 1904.
   viii, 509p.   20cm.
                              000

Added entries

The Queen's quair
The Six years' tragedy

COMMENT
Rule 1 again for the author entry. Inclusion of the alternative title
covered by rule 133E. Added entry under main title covered by rule
33P, and alternative title by rule 33P6, second paragraph.

EXAMPLE NO 3

Main entry

BUTLER, Samuel, 1835-1902
   Samuel Butler's notebooks: selections; edited by
Geoffrey Keynes and Brian Hill. London: Cape, 1951
(1952 reprint).
   327p.   20cm.

ooo

Added entries

KEYNES, Geoffrey, *ed.*
HILL, Brian, *ed.*

COMMENT

Entry under Butler for the main entry is covered by rule 1— ' Enter
... selections from works by one author under the person ... that is
the author.' Dates would have to be added to the heading to distinguish this Samuel Butler from the author of ' Hudibras ', who had
the same name (rule 52). Added entries would be necessary under the
editors. In the imprint the British rule has been followed, i.e. the
earliest date of the edition has been stated, and not the date of
reprinting, but the latter has been added in parentheses according to
the provisions of rule 142A. The author's name has been retained at
the beginning of the title, as there is nothing in the code to suggest it
should be omitted (see the third example to rule 134). As this method
hides what should be the filing element after the author's name the
uniform title device could be employed to obtain a better filing
sequence:
   BUTLER, Samuel, 1835-1902
   [Notebooks]. Samuel Butler's notebooks ...

EXAMPLE NO 4

Main entry

VILLCHUR, Edgar
   Reproduction of sound ...   Cambridge (Mass.): Acoustic
research; New York: Dover, c1965.
   [4], 92p.; illus.   22cm.
   "A revised and enlarged republication of the work
first published by Acoustic Research Inc. in 1962."

ooo

Straightforward author entry covered by rule 1 again. The presence of two publishers and two places of publication in the imprint is dealt with in rule 139B. The copyright date is the only date given, and this is indicated by a superior c before the date. This is dealt with by rule 142G. The use of the superior c is shown in the examples to rule 141G of the North American text. The four unnumbered pages are not accounted for by the numbered pages, and should be given in the collation in square brackets.

EXAMPLE NO 5

Main entry

LEWIS, C. S.
   English literature in the sixteenth century, excluding drama . . .
Oxford: Clarendon press, 1954 (1962 reprint).
   vi, [2], 696p. 22cm. (The Clark lectures, 1944; Oxford history of English literature, no. III).

ooo

Added entries

The Clark lectures, 1944
Oxford history of English literature, no III

COMMENT
Again, straightforward personal authorship covered by rule 1. The name of the series is, however, included in the title. This would be excluded from the title transcript by the provisions of rule 144D. On the page facing the title-page there is the name of another series. Thus we have two. This situation is catered for by rule 144GI—both would go in the series statement. The pagination calls for some comment. Of the three unnumbered pages, the last must be on the recto of page 2 of the second sequence. It is accounted for by the existing pagination, and therefore only [2] would go in square brackets. Added entries would be made under both series separately.

Main entry

KILPATRICK, Franklin P.
  The image of the Federal service, [by] Franklin P.
Kilpatrick, Milton C. Cummings, jr., [and] M. Kent
Jennings. Washington, D.C.: The Brookings institution,
1964.
  xvii, 301p. 23cm.

ooo

Added entries

CUMMINGS, Milton C., *jr.*
JENNINGS, M. Kent
The Image of the Federal service

COMMENT
Rule 3B1—Works of shared authorship, where the principal author is
not indicated, and there are not more than three authors, enter under
the first-named, and make added entries under the others. Reasonable
argument for a title added entry.

EXAMPLE NO 7

Main entry

SWANSON, Carl P.
  Cytogenetics, [by] Carl P. Swanson, Timothy Merz,
[and] William J. Young . . . Englewood Cliffs: Prentice-Hall,
c1967.
  xii, 194p.; illus., facsim. 23cm.
  References at the end of each chapter

ooo

Added entries

MERZ, Timothy
YOUNG, William J.

COMMENT
Rule 3B1 again. This time no title added entry required, as this would
be covered by a subject added entry.

EXAMPLE NO 8

Main entry

PERSISTENCE and change: Bennington College and its
   students after twenty-five years, by Theodore M.
   Newcomb . . . [and others]. New York, London: Wiley [1967],
   viii, [2], 292p. 23cm.
   Other authors are: Kathryn E. Koenig, Richard Flacks,
and Donald P. Warwick.

ooo

Added entry

NEWCOMB, Theodore M.

COMMENT
Works by more than three authors in which no author is represented
as the principal author are to be entered under their titles (rule 3B2).
Added entry is only to be made under the author named first on the
title-page.

EXAMPLE NO 9

Main entry

HARTNOLL, Phyllis, *ed.*
   Shakespeare in music: essays by John Stevens [and
others], with a catalogue of musical works. Edited by
Phyllis Hartnoll. London: Macmillan, 1964.
   ix, 333p. 22cm.
   Contents: Shakespeare and the music of the Elizabethan
stage, by John Stevens.—Song and part-song settings of
Shakespeare's lyrics, by Charles Cudworth.—Shakespeare and
the opera, by Winton Dean.— Shakespeare in the concert hall,
by Roger Fiske.—Catalogue of musical works based on the plays
and poetry of Shakespeare; compiled by Winton Dean, Dorothy
Moore, and Phyllis Hartnoll.

ooo

Added entry

SHAKESPEARE in music

Analytical entries

STEVENS, John
Shakespeare and the music of the Elizabethan
stage (*in* HARTNOLL, Phyllis, *ed*. Shakespeare in
music, 1964, pp. 3-48).

ooo

Similar entries would be made under the other contributors.

DEAN, Winton, *comp*.
Catalogue of musical works based on the plays and
poetry of Shakespeare; compiled by Winton Dean, Dorothy
Moore and Phyllis Hartnoll (*in* HARTNOLL, Phyllis, *ed*.
Shakespeare in music, pp. 243-290).

ooo

COMMENT
A work of multiple authorship produced under editorial direction—
rule 4A. Entry is under editor, as provided for in the rule, the editor
being named on the title-page. As there are more than three contributors, only the first would be mentioned in the title transcript,
followed by ' and others '. Normally the other contributors would be
mentioned in a note after the entry, but the importance of the
contributions would suggest the need for a contents note—see rule
145C9, and analytical entries under the authors' names (rule 33M).
One of these has been given in full, the others would be given similarly.
At least one analytical entry would be required for the catalogue of
musical works. Analytical entries under the titles of the separate
contributions would seem unnecessary. Subject analytical entries
would appear to be more appropriate.

EXAMPLE NO 10

Main entry

TROTMAN-DICKENSON, A. F.
Chemical kinetics, by A. F. Trotman-Dickenson . . .
[and] Surface and colloid chemistry, by G. D. Parfitt . . .
Oxford: Pergamon, [1966].
x, 170p. plate; illus.   20cm.   (Commonwealth and
international library, Intermediate chemistry division).
Bibl. p. 164.

ooo

Added entries and reference

PARFITT, G. D.
Surface and colloid chemistry (*in* TROTMAN-DICKENSON,
A. F. Chemical kinetics, pp. 75-170, [1966]).

ooo

COMMONWEALTH and international library, Intermediate
chemistry division

DICKENSON, A. F. Trotman-
See TROTMAN-DICKENSON, A. F.

COMMENT
A collection without a collective title is covered by rule 5B, by which
entry is to be made under the heading appropriate to the work listed
first on the title-page. The example to the rule would indicate the
need for an author/title analytical entry under the second author.
Series entry also seems called for here, and obviously a reference from
the second part of the compound name.

EXAMPLE NO II

Main entry

PÆDAGOGICA EVROPAEA: the European yearbook of
educational research ... Published with the
support of the Council for cultural
cooperation of the Council of Europe ...
1965. First volume ... Amsterdam and Brussels:
Agon Elsevier; Braunschweig: Westermann, [1965].
xii, 284p. 25cm.
Sub-titles also in French and German.

ooo

COMMENT

The cataloguing of serials is covered by rule 6, *ie* entry is generally under title. Rule 133 covers the recording of a title, and 133C deals with titles in more than one language—' If the title-page bears titles in two or more languages the first title is recorded.' If a subsequent title was in English this would also be recorded, but as the first title is in this case in English, this should be adequate. Added entries have not been made under the sub-titles because they are sub-titles, but their presence has been indicated on the main entry by a note. The 1965 on the title-page indicates the year covered by the volume, and so an imprint date must be supplied in square brackets.

EXAMPLE NO 12

Main entry

HURT, Peyton
Bibliography and footnotes: a style manual for
college and university students, by Peyton Hurt; revised
and enlarged by Mary L. Hurt Richmond ... Berkeley and
Los Angeles: University of California, c1949 (1963).
xii, 167p. 21cm.
References, pp. 155-6.

Added entry

RICHMOND, Mary L. Hurt, *rev.*

COMMENT

Rule 14 covers revisions. Obviously ' primary responsibility' in this instance still rests with the original author. The copyright date has been given in the imprint, followed by the date of printing (according to rule 142 in the British text—a copyright date under an earlier copyright convention is given in the imprint . . . and there is no evidence that the text is a later edition). The North American text would merely give 1963. An added entry is obviously needed under the reviser.

Main entry

MORTON, J. B.
    The best of Beachcomber [pseud.]; selected
and introduced by Michael Frayn. Harmondsworth:
Penguin, 1966.
    256p. 18cm.
    First pub. 1963.

ooo

Added entry and reference

FRAYN, Michael, *ed.*
BEACHCOMBER
    See MORTON, J. B.

COMMENT
Pseudonymous works are covered by rule 42. J B Morton used both
his pseudonym and his real name on title-pages of different works, and
thus should be entered under his real name. Rule 121A1 indicates
that a reference is to be made from the pseudonym to the real name.
An added entry would be needed under Frayn. A title added entry
would not be necessary.

EXAMPLE NO 14

Main entry

HANCOCK, Leslie
    Word index to James Joyce's Portrait of the artist
[as a young man] . . . Carbondale, Edwardsville: Southern Illinois
university press; London, Amsterdam: Feffer & Simons, c1967.
    ix, [2], 145p. 23cm.

Added entry

JOYCE, James: Portrait of the artist

COMMENT
This title is covered by rule 19—Related works, and more particularly
by 19B, for works not related to any particular edition of the original
work. Thus main entry is under its own author and title, with added
entry under the author and title of the work to which it is related. The
pagination may give some difficulty. Of the five unnumbered pages,
one is accounted for by page ix, *ie* it is on the verso, and the last two
of the five are allowed for by the main pagination starting with page 3.
Thus the number of unnumbered pages is two. In a modern book an
odd number of unnumbered pages would be extremely rare.

87

EXAMPLE NO 15

Main entry

T.L.S. 1962 : essays and reviews from The
  Times literary supplement. London :
  Oxford university press, 1963.
  viii, 240p. 22cm.

ooo

Added entry

The Times literary supplement

COMMENT

Extracts from periodicals are not covered by a specific rule in this
code. They are included within rule 19—Related works. As in the
previous example, rule 19B would apply, and the work entered under
its own author or title according to the general rules. An added entry
would be made under the title of the work to which it is related.

EXAMPLE NO 16

Main entry

STRINDBERG, August
  [Tjanslekvinnans son. English]. The son of
a servant : the story of the evolution of a human
being, 1849-67; newly translated with an
introduction and notes, by Evert Sprinchorn.
London : Cape, 1967.
  223p. 20cm.

ooo

Added entries and references

TJANSLEKVINNANS son
SPRINCHORN, Evert, *tr.*
STRINDBERG, August
  The son of a servant
  See his Tjanslekvinnans son. English
The SON of a servant
  See TJANSLEKVINNANS son. English

COMMENT

Another example of a related work, this time a translation. Translations are to be entered under their original authors by rule 15. The
problem of the original and translated titles is also involved. These
are covered by rules 101A and 105, as indicated in example 17 below.

88

Main entry

SCHRAMM, Werner
[Chemische und biologische Laboratorien. English].
Chemistry and biology laboratories: design—construction—
equipment, by Werner Schramm; [translated from the] 2nd
rev. and supplemented German ed. Translation ed. J. M.
Leytham: translator Mrs. M. Jansen. Oxford: Pergamon,
1965.
ix, 255p.; 787 illus. 28cm.
                              000

Reference

SCHRAMM, Werner
Chemistry and biology laboratories
See his Chemische und biologische Laboratorien. English

COMMENT
Translations are covered by rule 15 for entry, *ie* under the author
of the original work. No added entry is necessary under the translator
(see rule 33E). Translations also involve the rule for uniform titles.
This is a modern work, published after 1500, so entry is under the
original title (rule 101A), and rule 105 indicates that the name of the
language into which the translation is made should be added after the
uniform title. The author/title reference from the English title is
covered by rule 124.

EXAMPLE NO 18

Main entry

GIBBS-SMITH, Charles
... a directory and nomenclature of the first
aeroplanes, 1809-1909. London: H.M.S.O., 1966.
xi, 120p. 25cm.
At head of t.-p.: Science Museum.
                              000

Added entries and references

SCIENCE MUSEUM, *London*
SMITH, Charles Gibbs-
 See GIBBS-SMITH, Charles
LONDON. Science Museum.
 See SCIENCE MUSEUM, *London*

COMMENT
An example of corporate versus personal authorship covered by rules
17A and 17B. 17A states that reports by individual persons, even if
they are officers of the corporate body, as Gibbs-Smith is, would be
entered under the personal author. An added entry would also be
made under the corporate body. The omission of ' Science Museum '
from the start of the title transcript is indicated by three dots.
' Science Museum ' is given as a note after the entry to make the
added entry self-explanatory.

EXAMPLE NO 19

Main entry

UNITED STATES. *Copyright Office*
 Copyright law of the United States of America ...
Washington, D.C.: Library of Congress, 1967.
 iv, 87p. 23cm. (Bulletin no. 14, rev. to Jan. 1,
1967).

OOO

References

COPYRIGHT OFFICE. United States
 See UNITED STATES. *Copyright Office*
LIBRARY OF CONGRESS. *Copyright Office*
 See UNITED STATES. *Copyright Office*

COMMENT
This is an example of single authorship by a corporate body, therefore rule 1 would apply. Rule 70, *Other subordinate bodies* would
suggest entry of the Copyright Office under its own name, and not
under Library of Congress. As this, however, is a legislative docu-

ment, entry would be under United States, as indicated by rule 78B (see introduction to rule). A reference, of course, would be required from the name of the office.

EXAMPLE NO 20

Main entry

NEW rules for an old game : proceedings of a workshop
on the 1967 Anglo-American cataloguing code held
by the School of librarianship, the University of
British Columbia, April 13 and 14, 1967. Edited
by Thelma E. Allen [and] Daryl Ann Dickman. London :
Bingley, 1968.
175p. 23cm.
First pub. 1967 by the University of British Columbia
Bibl., pp. 161-165.

ooo

Added entries

ALLEN, Thelma E., *ed.*
DICKMAN, Daryl Ann, *ed.*
UNIVERSITY OF BRITISH COLUMBIA. *School of Librarianship*

COMMENT
The proceedings of a conference here entered by rule 87 under the name of the conference, which is distinctive enough for entry. This is also an example of a title-page spread over two facing pages, covered by rule 132A1—the information being transcribed as if from one page, without square brackets.

EXAMPLE NO 21

Main entry

LONGFORD, Frank Pakenham, *Earl*
 . . . five lives, [by] Frank Pakenham,
earl of Longford. London : Hutchinson,
c1964.
 279p.; port. 21cm.

ooo

Added entry and reference

FIVE lives
PAKENHAM, Frank, *Earl of Longford*
    See LONGFORD, Frank Pakenham, *Earl*

COMMENT

Rule 1 for authorship. Noblemen covered by rule 47—entry under the title of nobility.

EXAMPLE NO 22

Main entry

DAY, *Sir* Archibald
    ... the Admiralty hydrographic service, 1795-1919,
by Vice-Admiral Sir Archibald Day ... London: H.M.S.O.,
1967.
    378p., plates; fold. charts, facsim., col. maps. 25cm.
    At head of t.-p.: Ministry of Defence.
    A continuation of L. S. Dawson's ' Memoirs of hydrography ',
Pts. I & II, 1885.

ooo

Added entries and references

GREAT BRITAIN. *Ministry of Defence*
DAWSON, L. S. Memoirs of hydrography, Pts. I & II, 1885
The ADMIRALTY hydrographic service.
MINISTRY OF DEFENCE
    See GREAT BRITAIN. *Ministry of Defence*
DEFENCE, Ministry of
    See GREAT BRITAIN. *Ministry of Defence*
GREAT BRITAIN. *Admiralty*
    See also GREAT BRITAIN. *Ministry of Defence*

COMMENT

The choice between corporate and personal authorship presented here is fairly easily solved—rule 17A. Single reports made by officers of a corporate body are excluded from corporate authorship, unless written by more than three persons. An added entry would be made under the corporate body. The rule for related works (rule 19) is also involved. This would be covered by rule 19B, and be entered under its own author and title, with an added entry under the author/title of the work to which it is related. An added entry under the title would also seem to be useful here. References would be required from Ministry of Defence, and a *See also* from Great Britain. *Admiralty.* There will be entries under this heading for the period up to 1st April, 1964, when the Admiralty was abolished and absorbed into the Ministry of Defence.

EXAMPLE NO 23

Main entry

TANNER, J. C.
    ... 50-point traffic census—the first five
years, by J. C. Tanner ... and J. R. Scott ... London :
H.M.S.O., 1962.
    vi, 38p.; illus. 25cm. (Road research technical
paper, no. 63).
    At head of t.-p. : Department of Scientific and
Industrial Research. Road Research Laboratory.

ooo

Added entries and references

SCOTT, J. R.
ROAD RESEARCH LABORATORY
ROAD research technical paper, no. 63
50-point traffic census
GREAT BRITAIN. *Road Research Laboratory*
   See ROAD RESEARCH LABORATORY
GREAT BRITAIN. *Department of Scientific and Industrial Research.*
                   Road Research Laboratory
   See ROAD RESEARCH LABORATORY

COMMENT
Again covered by rule 17A. Scientific reports by two officers would be catalogued under the first named and added entry made under Road Research Laboratory. This would be entered directly under its own name as type 2 listed under rule 78A. An added entry under the second author would be needed, and a title added entry would also be useful. References would be required from the other forms of name by which the Laboratory might be sought.

EXAMPLE NO 24

Main entry

GREAT BRITAIN. *Scottish Health Services Council*
    ... administrative practice of hospital boards in Scotland:
report by a committee of the Scottish health services council.
Edinburgh: H.M.S.O., 1966.
    109p. 25cm.
    W. M. Farquharson-Lang, *chairman*
ooo

References

SCOTTISH HEALTH SERVICES COUNCIL
    See GREAT BRITAIN. *Scottish Health Services Council*
GREAT BRITAIN. *Scottish Home and Health Department. Scottish*
                 Health Services Council
    See GREAT BRITAIN. *Scottish Health Services Council*
SCOTTISH Home and Health Department
    See GREAT BRITAIN. *Scottish Home and Health Department*
SCOTLAND. *Home and Health Department*
    See GREAT BRITAIN. *Scottish Home and Health Department*
FARQUHARSON-LANG, W. M., *chairman*
    See GREAT BRITAIN. *Scottish Health Services Council*

COMMENT

A government body which is covered by rule 78 B, and would therefore be entered under the name of the government. The Scottish
Health Services Council is a subordinate agency, but would be entered
directly under the name of the country by rule 79A. Scottish libraries
might prefer a more direct heading—Scotland. *Health Services Council*. The need for references from different forms of citation of the
name of the body is indicated by those given.

EXAMPLE NO 25

Main entry

GREAT BRITAIN. *Committee of Scientists on the scientific*
and technological aspects of the Torrey Canyon disaster
... the Torrey Canyon: report of the Committee of scientists
on the scientific and technological aspects of the Torrey
Canyon disaster. London: H.M.S.O., 1967.
viii, 47p., plates. 25cm.
At head of t.-p.: Cabinet Office.
Sir Solly Zuckerman, *chairman.*

ooo

References

COMMITTEE of Scientists on the scientific and technological
aspects of the Torrey Canyon disaster
See GREAT BRITAIN. *Committee of Scientists on the scientific and*
technological aspects of the Torrey Canyon disaster
GREAT BRITAIN. *Cabinet Office. Committee* etc.
See GREAT BRITAIN. *Committee* etc.
ZUCKERMAN, *Sir* Solly, *chairman*
See GREAT BRITAIN. *Committee* etc.

COMMENT
Same comment as for no 24. See also page 45 of text regarding
government publications.

28609